DECODABLE
BO
Take-Ho
Grade 2

Harcourt

Orlando   Boston   Dallas   Chicago   San Diego

Visit *The Learning Site!*

www.harcourtschool.com

Printed in the United States of America

Part number 9997-38088-6
ISBN 0-15-326768-2

7 8 9 10 085 10 09 08 07 06 05

Contents

BOOK 18

BOOK 19

BOOK 20

The County Park

by Terry Larkin

illustrated by Bradley Clark

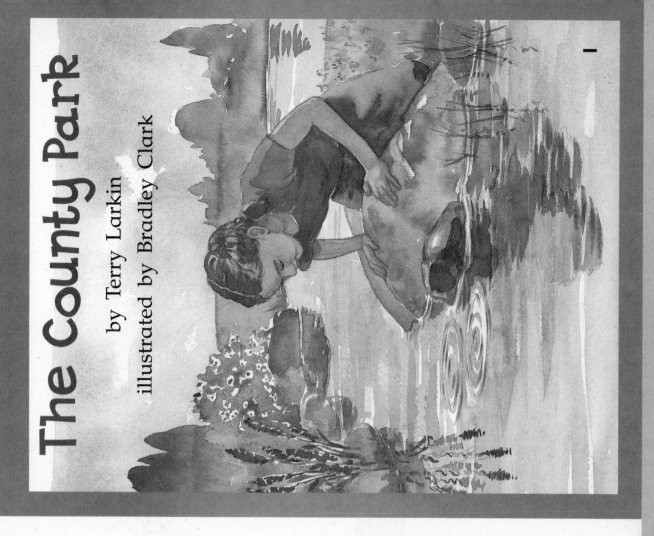

©Harcourt

DECODABLE BOOK 12
The County Park

I like my house, but I like to go outside even more. The county park is not far away, and I go there to hike around. I want to be a park ranger.

2

©Harcourt

(continued)

Decodable Words

on	sorry
or	splash
out	stand
outside	still
over	tadpole
park	that
peeking	the
perhaps	then
play	tracks
pond	turn
poundcake	up
ranger	watch
rocks	water
round	we
see	when
shout	will
sky	write
soon	your

I hear a splash in the pond. Perhaps it is fish or frogs jumping. When they are feeding, they come up to grab insects. I can hear the insects buzzing around me.

*Boldface words indicate sound-spelling introduced in this story.

3

The round circles in the water mark
the area to look. It was a tadpole I saw.
Soon he will turn into a frog.

"The County Park"

Word Count: 204

High-Frequency Words	**Decodable Words**	
about	a	he
animal	an	hear
animals	and	hike
are	at	home
around	be	**house**
away	but	hurt
blue	buzzing	I
come	can	in
into	circles	insects
look	**clouds**	inside
of	**county**	is
one	dog	it
saw	eat	jumping
there	even	later
they	far	leave
to	feeding	lie
want	fish	like
was	fly	little
what	**found**	mark
wonder	frog	me
you	frogs	more
	get	**mound**
	go	**mouse**
	grab	muddy
	grasshoppers	my
	ground	not

*Boldface words indicate sound-spelling introduced in this story.

I shout to my dog when I get home. "Sorry, Poundcake, later. I have to get my nature book. I want to write about the animals I found. Then we can play."

I see little tracks on the muddy ground. In that mound of rocks, there is an animal inside! It is like a mouse. I wonder what it is.

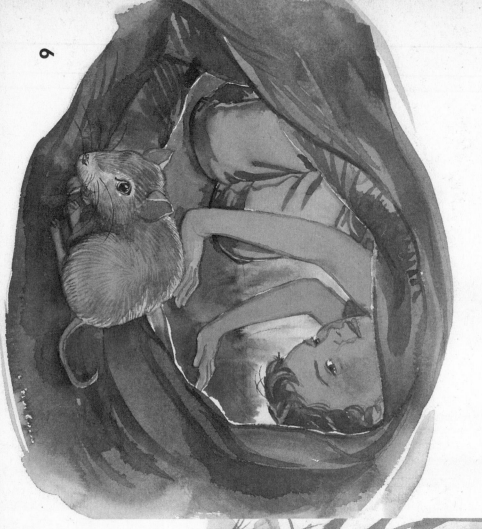

It is peeking out at me. I will not
hurt you, little one. You can leave
your house and come outside. I will
stand still.

Later I lie on the ground and watch
insects. I can look up in the blue sky
and watch clouds fly over. I wonder
what grasshoppers eat?

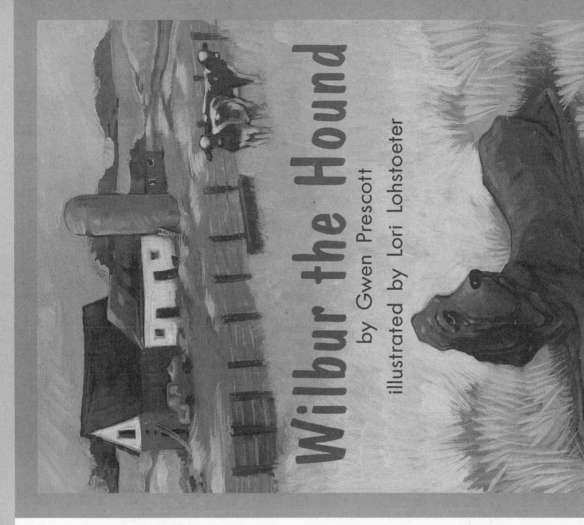

Wilbur the Hound

by Gwen Prescott

illustrated by Lori Lohstoeter

DECODABLE BOOK 12
Wilbur the Hound

Farmer Bill had a hound called Wilbur. Wilbur did not like changes. First, he lived inside the house with Farmer Bill. Later, he had to live outside in the barn.

2

(continued)

Now Wilbur had another change.
Farmer Bill was very proud of his new
cow. It lived in the barn with Wilbur,
who did not like to share. Wilbur
was grouchy.

Decodable Words

out	the
outside	track
perhaps	very
plan	walking
proud	way
sad	went
south	when
still	Wilbur
that	with
	yard

Boldface words indicate sound-spelling introduced in this story.

3

"Wilbur the Hound"
Word Count: 204

High-Frequency Words

another	
around	
do	
friend	
have	
lived	
looking	
new	
of	
one	
saw	
someday	
to	
was	
what	
where	
who	
worked	
would	

Decodable Words

a	get
and	glad
back	grazing
bad	**grouchy**
barn	**ground**
be	had
Bill	he
Bill's	headed
bounded	him
but	his
called	**hound**
change	**hounds**
changes	**house**
counting	in
cow	inside
crouched	it
day	later
did	like
down	live
farmer	**loud**
felt	mad
field	not
find	now
first	on
found	opened
gate	

*Boldface words indicate sound-spelling introduced in this story.

One day Wilbur was walking around the yard. He saw Farmer Bill's gate key on the ground. The key opened the gate to the field where the cow was grazing.

4

When the farmer was not looking, Wilbur opened the gate. He was glad the gate was not loud. The cow headed south. Wilbur felt proud that his plan had worked.

Farmer Bill was glad to have his cow back. Wilbur was still grouchy, but sharing the barn was not that bad. Perhaps someday the cow would be his friend.

Wilbur crouched down to get the scent. He would track the cow the way hounds do. He bounded out of the yard. Farmer Bill was counting on him.

Farmer Bill found out what Wilbur had done. He was sad and mad. Wilbur was not proud now. He went to find the cow.

6

7

Howard, My Twin

by Rose Howard

illustrated by Tom McKee

DECODABLE BOOK 12
Howard, My Twin

My name is Emily Powell. I have a twin brother, Howard. I'm the one with the long dark hair. Howard and I were rowdy when we were little.

(continued)

People always ask me how I like having a twin. Wow! I love it. Birthday parties are the best! We wear crowns, eat two cakes, and sing two times.

Decodable Words

name	stay
not	stick
now	team
older	teams
on	the
parties	thing
partner	things
perfect	time
play	times
Powell	twin
power	until
proud	up
rowdy	**vowed**
run	we
runs	went
same	when
sing	with
size	**wow**

*Boldface words indicate sound-spelling introduced in this story.

Another good thing about being a twin is having a partner. Howard was the perfect partner for the seesaw. He was my size. When he went up, I went down.

4

"Howard, My Twin"
Word Count: 207

High-Frequency Words

about
another
are
cook
do
friends
good
have
love
of
one
people
said
seesaw
to
today
two
was
were
working

Decodable Words

a	get
always	glad
and	he
as	hit
ask	hitter
back	home
ball	**how**
be	I
being	I'm
best	in
birthday	is
Bowser	it
cakes	it's
cheer	keep
chow	led
chowder	like
chowders	likes
clam	little
corn	long
crowd	made
crowns	may
down	me
eat	much
for	my
forth	

*Boldface words indicate sound-spelling introduced in this story.

What the Clown Sees

by Albert Pinsky

illustrated by Barbara Hranilovich

DECODABLE BOOK 12
What the Clown Sees

Our circus comes to a town, and the fun begins. The clowns have been getting ready all day. The sight of a happy crowd in the stands makes us glad.

2

(continued)

Down on the floor we start the march into the rings. The crowd looks at all the animals. The crowd watches the brown horses wearing green silk.

Decodable Words

like	roar
make	**rowdy**
makes	safe
march	see
mice	sees
miss	show
my	sight
not	silk
now	so
off	stands
on	start
or	take
our	the
over	time
partner	**town**
play	us
powder	we
powerful	wearing
ready	when
riding	with
rings	**wow**

*Boldface words indicate sound-spelling introduced in this story.

We do a funny dance close to the
lion. We can see his powerful legs
and hear him roar. We do not want
the people to frown. We are safe
from the lions.

4

"What the Clown Sees"

Word Count: 207

High-Frequency Words   **Decodable Words**

High-Frequency Words	Decodable Words		
animals	a	face	
are	all	floor	
comes	and	floppy	
do	at	**flower**	
doing	arm	**frown**	
from	before	fun	
give	begins	funny	
good	**brown**	getting	
have	but	glad	
into	cake	green	
look	can	happy	
of	clap	hat	
people	close	hear	
put	clothes	him	
some	**clown**	his	
to	**clown's**	horses	
want	**clowns**	I	
what	**crowd**	in	
you	**crowds**	is	
	cycles	it	
	dance	job	
	day	know	
	down	legs	
	dress	lift	

*Boldface words indicate sound-spelling introduced in this story.

We dress like mice so we can play with the elephant. Now it is time to give my partner some cake. I lift my arm.

Clowns see the crowds laugh and clap. We like you to have a good time. When the circus is over, we take off the funny clothes and face powder.

Wow! We look rowdy and funny,
but we know what we are doing.
You know a clown's job is to make
you laugh, so do not miss our show.

6

Riding cycles is fun. We do it over
and over before the show. We put
a floppy flower in our hat or make
a funny face and see you laugh.

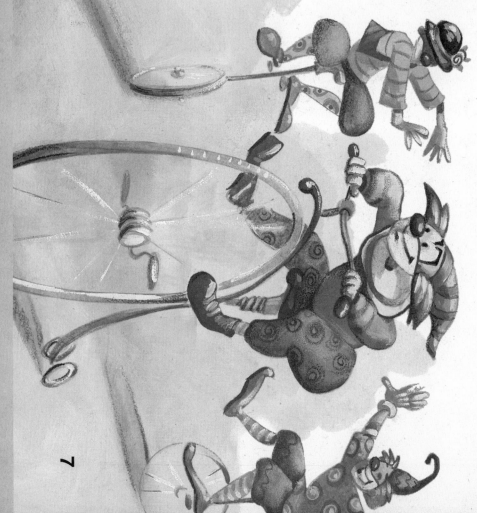

7

Chuck's Choice

by Dennis Gonzalez

illustrated by Stephen Lewis

DECODABLE BOOK 13
Chuck's Choice

Chuck and Becky took turns deciding what to do for the weekend. It was Chuck's choice to visit Uncle Bud's ranch. Uncle Bud liked to point out things at the ranch.

2

(continued)

Chuck and Becky stood on the noisy train platform. They didn't see Uncle Bud, but they heard his voice over all the noise.

"Chuck! Becky!" he called.

3

Decodable Words

noise	the
noisy	them
oink	then
on	things
out	till
over	time
pen	too
pig	tour
pigs	train
planting	turns
platform	uncle
point	under
pointed	us
ranch	visit
ready	**voice**
Rose	wait
see	walked
she	we
short	we'll
showed	we're
so	weekend
soil	went
soon	when
that	with

*Boldface words indicate sound-spelling introduced in this story.

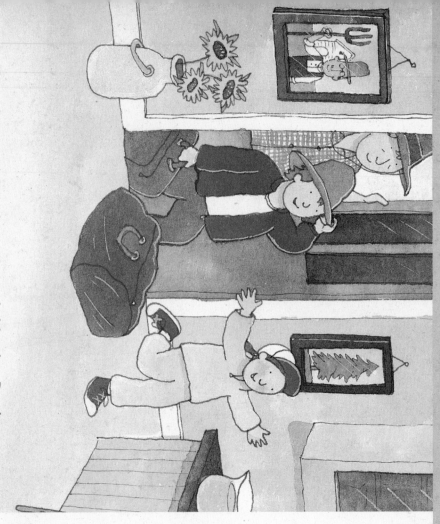

Chuck and Becky joined Uncle Bud.

At the ranch, Aunt Rose gave them a big hug.

"It's so nice to see you. I thought you were avoiding us," she said.

4

©Harcourt

"Chuck's Choice"
Word Count: 206
High-Frequency Words   **Decodable Words**

High-Frequency Words	Decodable Words	
come	a	don't
cook	all	**foil**
do	also	for
have	an	gave
of	and	go
put	asked	got
said	at	he
some	back	heard
they	Becky	his
thought	big	home
to	**boiled**	how
took	**broiler**	hug
was	**broiling**	I
were	Bud	in
what	Bud's	is
you	burgers	it
	but	it's
	called	**joined**
	choice	kids
	Chuck	liked
	Chuck's	little
	close	lunch
	corn	made
	dark	**moist**
	deciding	need
	didn't	nice

*Boldface words indicate sound-spelling introduced in this story.

Soon it was time to go home. Aunt Rose was disappointed that the visit was so short.

"Come back soon!" she called. "You don't need an appointment."

8

"Wait till you see what we made for lunch! We're broiling burgers. We'll put corn in foil and cook it under the broiler. We'll also have some boiled potatoes."

5

Uncle Bud went with the kids for a tour of the ranch. He pointed out how the soil was ready for planting.

"See how dark and moist it is?" he asked.

Then he walked them over to the pig pen. He showed them the noisy little pigs.

"Oink, oink," said the mother pig when Chuck and Becky got too close.

6

7

Moira's Voice

by Pat Burton

illustrated by Julie Durrell

1

DECODABLE BOOK 13
Moira's Voice

Moira had a very nice singing voice. She decided to join a singing group. Her first choice was called Cheerful Noises. However, she did not know where the singers practiced.

2

(continued)

One day her friend Holly saw a sign for Cheerful Noises. She called to Moira. "See this," she said pointing to the sign. "You need to make an appointment for a tryout."

Decodable Words

nice	song
noises	**spoiled**
not	stand
on	started
our	the
own	think
place	this
plenty	time
pointed	told
pointing	too
sang	tryout
seat	us
see	**voice**
she	**voices**
sign	wait
sing	we
singers	week
singing	will
so	with

*Boldface words indicate sound-spelling introduced in this story.

On the day of the tryout, she got on the bus. She gave some coins to the driver and found a seat. She got to her tryout in plenty of time.

Boldface words indicate sound-spelling introduced in this story.

"Moira's Voice"
Word Count: 206

High-Frequency Words

cheerful
friend
love
of
one
said
saw
should
some
to
was
where
you

Decodable Words

a	get
an	**Goines**
and	got
at	had
be	happy
better	help
bus	her
called	Holly
can't	hope
choice	hospital
coins	however
day	I
decided	I'd
did	in
dream	**join**
driver	know
feel	leader
fine	lifted
first	liked
for	make
found	met
Friday	need
gave	next

At the appointed time, Moira met the leader of Cheerful Noises. Mrs. Goines pointed to the place where she should stand. She told Moira to sing a song of her own choice.

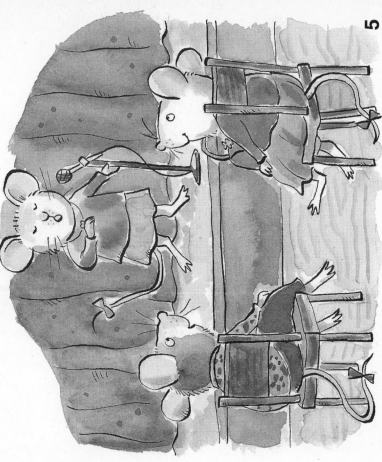

"I think so, too, Mrs. Goines. I can't wait to get started with Cheerful Noises."

"Fine, Moira. See you on Friday at practice!"

"I'd love to join," said Moira.

"We will be singing at the hospital next week," Mrs. Goines told her. "We think our happy voices help the patients feel better."

Moira lifted her voice and sang "The Spoiled Dream." Mrs. Goines liked her voice and her song.

"I hope you will join us, Moira," said Mrs. Goines.

Floyd
and His Oysters

by Norris Usher

illustrated by Patti Beling Murphy

DECODABLE BOOK 13
Floyd and His Oysters

The food Floyd likes best is oysters.
He could eat them every night.

"You are a strange boy," his sister Joyce told him. "I never saw a boy who enjoyed oysters so much."

(continued)

Decodable Words

might	sell
much	shelf
my	shell
never	sister
night	so
noodles	**soy**
on	**soybeans**
only	strange
oyster	talk
oysters	that
pearl	the
pearls	them
placed	then
raise	**toys**
replied	tried
right	trying
sand	use
say	with
	your

"Who are you to talk about being strange? You like to eat soybeans! You use soy sauce on everything! Even noodles!" said Floyd.

"You're right," said Joyce. "You can eat your oysters. I'll eat my soybeans."

*Boldface words indicate sound-spelling introduced in this story.

Floyd knew he wanted to be an oyster farmer. He would raise oysters and maybe even pearls. He would sell them at the Farmers' Market.

"Floyd and His Oysters"

Word Count: 224

High-Frequency Words

about	
again	
are	
around	
every	
everything	
looking	
of	
once	
said	
saw	
some	
these	
thought	
to	
wanted	
who	
would	
you	
you're	

Decodable Words

a	an	found
and	at	get
grain	be	grow
he	before	him
being	best	how
his	**boy**	I
box	I'll	if
bigger	can	in
change	inside	cried
destroy	is	it
eat	**Joyce**	just
enjoy	kept	
enjoyed		
enjoyment		
even	learned	like
farmer	lined	
farmers'	made	
Floyd	market	
food	maybe	

*Boldface words indicate sound-spelling introduced in this story.

"The only change I would enjoy is bigger oysters!"

"I said it before, and I'll say it again, Floyd," replied Joyce. "You are a strange boy!"

Floyd learned how oysters made pearls. If he placed a grain of sand inside the shell, that would annoy the oyster. Then the oyster would grow the pearl around the grain of sand.

Once Floyd found a pearl in an oyster.
He kept it in a box lined with corduroy.
Floyd kept the box on a shelf with his toys.
He enjoyed looking at it every day.

Joyce tried to get Floyd to enjoy some soybeans with his oysters.

"You're trying to destroy my enjoyment of these oysters!" Floyd cried.

Joyce said, "I just thought you might enjoy a change."

The Joyful Voyage

by Wilbur Glenn

illustrated by Bethann Thornburgh

1

DECODABLE BOOK 13
The Joyful Voyage

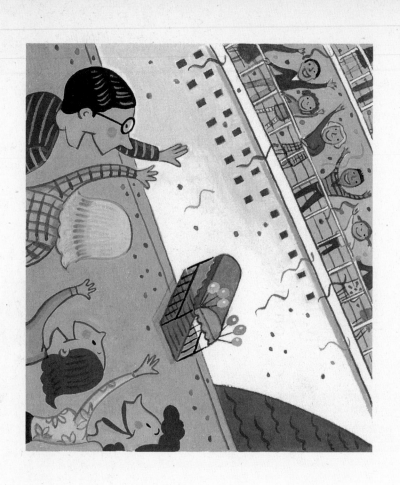

Troy Malloy and his sister, Joy, waved to the people on shore. They were going on a voyage. Five days on a ship! What would they do? Would they enjoy it?

2

(continued)

Even so, it was fun to wave good-bye. Troy and Joy felt like part of a royal family. It was fun to pretend that the people on shore were the loyal subjects.

Decodable Words

nearby	song
now	**soy**
on	subjects
out	swimming
oysters	tea
pants	that
part	the
played	then
pool	this
pools	those
pretend	three
rice	told
room	trip
royal	**Troy**
sat	watching
sea	wave
she	waved
ship	waving
shore	we
shouted	went
sights	when
sipping	will
sister	with
smiled	
so	

Boldface words indicate sound-spelling introduced in this story.

Troy and Joy's grandparents were on the shore, waving. They shouted, "Enjoy the trip! Be a good boy, Troy! Be a good girl, Joy."

4

"The Joyful Voyage"
Word Count: 226

High-Frequency Words

do
evening
family
good
great
have
nothing
of
people
said
they
to
was
were
what
would

Decodable Words

a	girl
adding	go
all	going
and	grandparents
asked	had
at	him
band	his
be	in
boy	it
bye	**Joy**
can	**Joy's**
change	**joyful**
day	**joyfully**
days	jumped
destroy	like
dining	**loyal**
each	main
enjoy	**Malloy**
enjoyed	**Malloys**
enjoyment	maybe
even	member
felt	mom
five	mood
found	more
four	my
fun	

*Boldface words indicate sound-spelling introduced in this story.

©Harcourt

"Maybe this will be fun after all," said Troy. When the ship was out at sea, the Malloy family enjoyed the sights. Then Troy asked his mom, "What can we do now?"

That evening, the Malloys went to the dining room. Each member of the Malloy family had oysters and rice with soy sauce. "What a great day!" said Troy. "We have four more days to go. Oh, boy!"

"Change out of those corduroy pants and go swimming!" his mom told him. "Enjoy the trip!"

So Troy and Joy went swimming. The ship had three pools. They found the main pool and jumped in.

Mr. and Mrs. Malloy sat nearby, sipping tea and watching. A band played a joyful song, adding to the enjoyment. "Nothing can destroy my good mood," said Mrs. Malloy. She smiled joyfully.

COOPER'S COOL IDEA

by Grant Birch

illustrated by Mary Bono

DECODABLE BOOK 14
Cooper's Cool Idea

Cooper was in the mood for a cool treat. He said, "Let's see if Booth wants some ice cream."

Cooper went over to Booth's house. "Come on, Booth," he called. "Let's get some ice cream."

2

(continued)

Decodable Words

no	see
noon	shop
on	silly
opens	**soon**
out	the
outside	them
over	then
owner	told
please	treat
pool	walked
red	went
replied	when
rid	will
right	with
Scooby	**Woo**
scoop	

"OK," said Booth. "I'll put on my boots.
I'll be right back." Cooper and his dog,
Scooby, knew about Booth and his red
cowboy boots. Booth liked to wear them
when he went out.

3

*Boldface words indicate sound-spelling introduced in this story.

Soon Booth came outside, holding two balloons. He gave a balloon to his friend. Then the boys walked to the ice cream shop.

"What will you have, Cooper?" asked Mr. Woo, the owner.

4

"Cooper's Cool Idea"
Word Count: 215

High-Frequency Words

about	
come	
friend	
great	
have	
idea	
of	
one	
put	
said	
school	
some	
their	
they	
to	
two	
wants	
was	
were	
what	
you	

Decodable Words

a	go	
and	hands	
as	he	
asked	him	
at	his	
back	holding	
barked	house	
be	how	
Booth	I'll	
Booth's	I'm	
boots	ice	
boys	if	
called	in	
came	is	
cones	it	
cool	jumped	
Cooper	just	
Cooper's	last	
cowboy	left	
cream	let's	
dog	liked	
fool	**mood**	
for	my	
gave	never	
get	next	
gloomy		

*Boldface words indicate sound-spelling introduced in this story.

"A scoop of strawberry," said Cooper.

"How about you, Booth?" asked Mr. Woo.

"A scoop of chocolate, please," replied Booth.

"What will you have, Scooby?" asked Mr. Woo. Scooby just barked.

Soon the boys were at the pool. "Last one in is a silly fool!" the boys called as they jumped in.

The boys left the shop with ice-cream cones in their hands.

"You have great ideas, Cooper," Booth told him. "I'm never gloomy when I'm with you. What's next?"

"Let's go to the pool at the school. It opens at noon. You will have to get rid of the red boots. No boots in the pool!" said Cooper.

The Tool Room

by Allen York

illustrated by Kristin Barr

1

DECODABLE BOOK 14
The Tool Room

Dan liked to work with his granddad's tools. When he visited his granddad, they would fix things around the house.

One day, Dan saw something oozing out from under his granddad's sink.

2

"See that, Granddad?" he asked. "What would make water ooze out like that?"

"Well, Dan," replied Granddad. "I think something might be loose. Let's go to the tool room."

(continued)

Decodable Words

own	think
perfect	thinking
pipe	this
place	tighten
replied	tiles
right	**tool**
roof	**tools**
room	tying
sanders	under
say	visited
see	visiting
seeing	water
sink	we
smoothing	well
so	when
soon	will
sounds	wire
spools	wrench
stopped	**zoo**
that	
the	
things	

*Boldface words indicate sound-spelling introduced in this story.

3

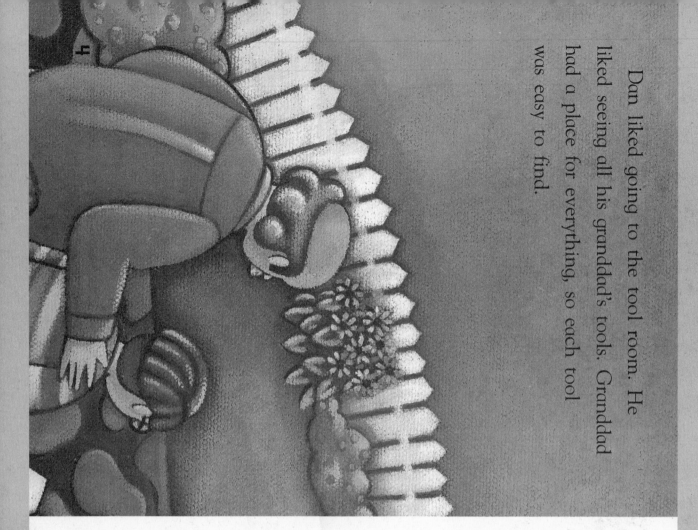

Dan liked going to the tool room. He liked seeing all his granddad's tools. Granddad had a place for everything, so each tool was easy to find.

4

"The Tool Room"
Word Count: 219

High-Frequency Words	Decodable Words	
about	a	grow
around	all	had
do	also	hammers
everything	and	he
from	asked	help
great	be	his
looked	Dan	house
of	Dan's	I
one	day	in
said	each	is
saw	easy	kept
should	favorites	leak
something	find	let's
there	fix	like
these	fixed	liked
they	fixing	**loose**
to	**food**	make
today	for	might
was	gardening	nails
were	get	now
what	go	on
work	going	**ooze**
would	granddad	**oozing**
you	granddad's	out

*Boldface words indicate sound-spelling introduced in this story.

©Harcourt

Granddad kept his gardening tools in the tool room. These were Dan's favorites. He liked to help Granddad grow his own food.

"Let's find a tool to fix the pipe," said Granddad.

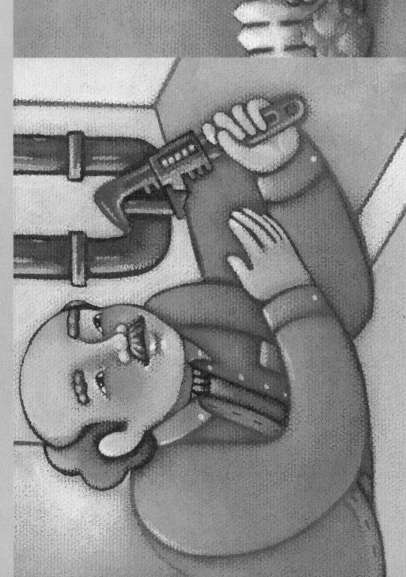

Soon Granddad had fixed the leak. The water stopped oozing from the pipe.

"Great, Granddad! Now what should we do?"

"Well, I was thinking about visiting the zoo. What do you say?"

"Sounds perfect. Let's go!"

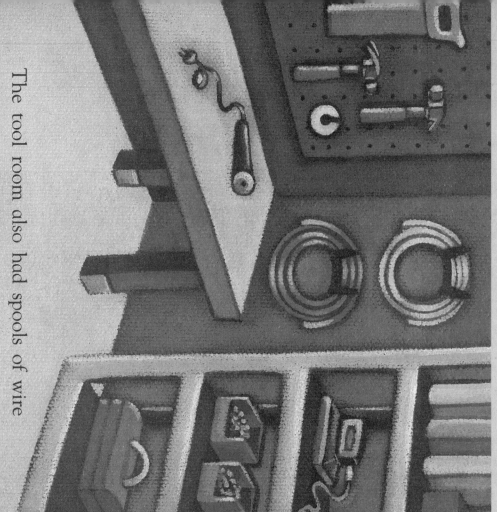

The tool room also had spools of wire for tying things. There were sanders for smoothing wood. There were hammers and nails for fixing loose tiles on the roof.

Today, they looked for a tool to tighten a loose pipe. Granddad knew the right one to get.

"This is a wrench," he said. "This tool will fix that loose pipe."

A True Test

by Cathy Finch

illustrated by Lauren Scheuer

DECODABLE BOOK 14
A True Test

Sue Ann put on her best blue jeans and got ready for school. Then she went down to breakfast. She put cereal and milk into her blue bowl and sat down to eat.

(continued)

"How about some blueberries on that cereal, Sue Ann?" asked her mom.

"That would be nice," said Sue Ann.

"Blueberries taste great with breakfast."

Decodable Words

later	study	
liked	**Sue**	
me	taste	
met	test	
milk	that	
mom	the	
next	then	
nice	this	
no	time	
on	told	
out	**true**	
outside	up	
ready	visiting	
recess	walk	
remind	walked	
replied	went	
sat	when	
she	window	
	with	

*Boldface words indicate sound-spelling introduced in this story.

Sue Ann looked out the window. A bluebird was visiting the bird feeder. Sue Ann always felt happy when she saw the bluebirds. She had a feeling this would be a great day.

4

©Harcourt

"A True Test"

Word Count: 230

High-Frequency Words	Decodable Words	
about	a	eat
are	always	false
coming	and	feeder
do	Ann	feeding
friend	Ann's	felt
good	as	fine
great	ask	for
have	asked	forgot
into	at	glad
looked	be	got
put	best	Greg
said	bird	had
saw	**blue**	happy
school	**bluebirds**	her
some	**bluebird**	how
they	**blueberries**	I
to	bowl	I'll
today	breakfast	if
together	**bluebirds**	is
was	called	it
what	cried	it's
would	day	jeans
you	deal	just
	did	know
	didn't	known
	down	

*Boldface words indicate sound-spelling introduced in this story.

Sue Ann's friend Greg met her outside. They liked to walk to school together.

"Are you ready for the test today?" asked Sue Ann as they walked.

"What test?" asked Greg.

"Didn't you study?" asked Sue Ann.

"I did just fine."

"Good for you, Sue Ann!" said Greg. "Next time a test is coming up, I'll ask you to remind me."

"It's a deal, Greg," said Sue Ann.

"Oh, no," cried Greg. "I forgot!"

"If I had known, I would have called to remind you," replied Sue Ann.

"I know you would have," said Greg. "You are a true-blue friend."

Later that day, Sue Ann and Greg met at recess. "How did you do on the test?" asked Sue Ann.

"I was glad it was a true or false test," Greg told her. "How did you do?"

True-Blue Friend

by Helen Archer

illustrated by Tammy Smith

DECODABLE BOOK 14
True-Blue Friend

"I don't have a clue how to begin," whined Lester.

"What's the matter?" asked Sue, holding a blue crayon in her hand.

"I don't know how to draw a blue jay."

2

(continued)

Sue and Lester were working on an art project. They were trying to show a forest with living things in it. Sue used cut paper to make her picture.

Decodable Words

out	thanks
part	that
project	that's
rabbits	the
replied	them
robins	then
seems	things
she	told
show	trees
side	**true**
spruce	trying
started	used
Sue	whined
talent	will
talents	with
tall	your

She had bluebells and other pretty flowers on one side of the picture. She had spruce trees in another part. Sue had made them look tall.

"True-Blue Friend"

Word Count: 215

High-Frequency Words	Decodable Words		
another	a	had
are	add	hand
could	all	has
everyone	an	he
friend	and	her
have	art	holding
here's	asked	how
look	be	I
of	begin	I'll
one	**blue**	if
other	**bluebells**	in
paper	can	it
picture	**clue**	it's
pictures	crayon	jay
pretty	cut	jays
said	deer	just
they	deserve	know
to	different	Lester
were	don't	made
what's	fine	make
working	finish	matter
you	flowers	mine
	for	my
	forest	needed
	glad	not
	glue	on

*Boldface words indicate sound-spelling introduced in this story.

©Harcourt

In the trees, she had blue jays and robins. All she needed to add were deer and rabbits. Lester, on the other hand, had barely started. He told Sue that he could not draw.

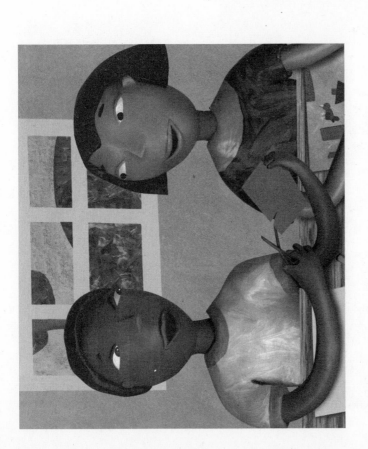

"Don't worry, Lester. Everyone has different talents. If you cut out pictures and glue them to the paper, your art will be fine."

"Sue, you are a true-blue friend," said Lester.

"That's OK, Lester," said Sue. "Here's a clue. You don't have to draw the art. You can cut out the pictures. Then glue them to the paper."

"Thanks, Sue, for the clue. You deserve a blue ribbon for your art. I'll just be glad if I can finish mine!"

"It's true that my talent seems to be art," replied Sue.

Forest Review

by Dana Catharine

illustrated by Stacey Schuett

One morning Andrew and Jenny were walking in the cool forest. The dew was still on the leaves. They listened to the new sounds! They heard the crunch of their feet on the fallen leaves. What was that?

2

(continued)

©Harcourt

Decodable Words

not	swam
on	tail
our	that
own	the
peck	thump
pond	tree
sat	up
singing	very
sound	walking
sounds	we
sticks	wind
still	with

Thump, thump, thump!
Andrew and Jenny saw a pond.
In the pond swam a few beavers.
One was carrying sticks in his
mouth. One was beating the sticks
with her tail.

Croak, croak, croak!
What was that? In the pond
Andrew and Jenny viewed a frog.
He was catching bugs and
singing. Crack! The frog jumped
into the pond!

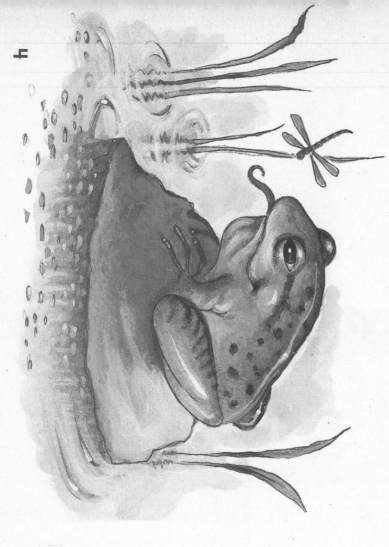

©Harcourt

"Forest Review"
Word Count: 222
High-Frequency Words

	Decodable Words	
animals	a	feet
away	and	**few**
into	**Andrew**	**flew**
listen	as	for
listened	asked	forest
looked	beating	frog
looking	beaver	**grew**
of	beavers	hands
one	**blew**	he
said	both	heard
saw	bugs	her
their	by	his
there	can	in
they	carrying	is
to	catching	it
was	children	Jenny
were	clap	jumped
what	clapped	**knew**
	cool	leaves
	crack	let's
	croak	like
	crunch	make
	dew	morning
	did	mouth
	fallen	**new**
	feather	

*Boldface words indicate sound-spelling introduced in this story.

Andrew and Jenny knew that animals did not like new forest sounds. The children grew very still. A feather blew by in the wind. What was that?

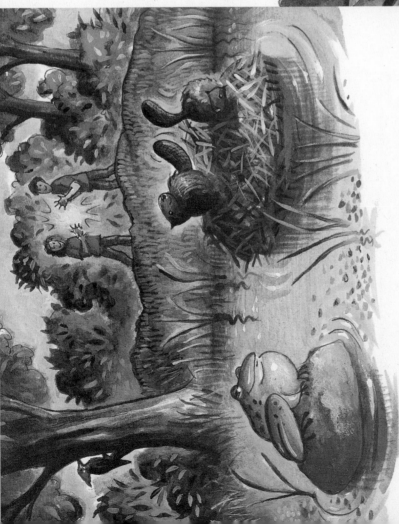

"Let's review the forest sounds," said Andrew. Thump, thump. That is the beaver! Croak, croak. That is the frog. Peck, peck. That is the woodpecker. Clap, clap. That is the echo of our hands.

Peck, Peck, Peck!

Andrew and Jenny looked up. There in a tree that grew by the pond sat a woodpecker. It was looking for bugs. Crack! The woodpecker flew away.

6

"We can make our own forest sound," said Andrew.

"What new sound can we make?" asked Jenny. "Listen to that echo." they both said as they clapped their hands. Clap, clap, clap!

7

Drew's Practice

by Dana Catharine

illustrated by John Wallace

1

DECODABLE BOOK 15
Drew's Practice

It was a sunny afternoon. The wind blew softly in the windows. Drew sat at the piano. Her fingers moved quickly up and down the keys. She was practicing her lesson.

(continued)

Artie and Kelly wanted to practice for their soccer game. They wanted Drew to play with them. Artie and Kelly knew that Drew was a good soccer player. It would be fun to play with Drew.

Decodable Words

on	the
out	them
outside	**threw**
play	tired
played	try
player	up
quickly	us
replied	wait
right	we
sat	when
she	while
soccer	will
softly	wind
strong	windows
sunny	with
tapped	your
that	

Boldface words indicate sound-spelling introduced in this story.

"Drew! Drew! Come out and practice with us!" called Artie and Kelly. "Come help us review the plays for the game! We need your help to practice."

"Drew's Practice"

Word Count: 234

High-Frequency Words	Decodable Words		
come	a	afternoon	**flew**
good	an	for	
great	and	fun	
have	Artie	game	
idea	at	gave	
moved	back	had	**grew**
moves	ball	hand	
said	bars	help	
they	be	her	
to	beat	hot	
want	bit	I	
wanted	**blew**	in	
was	bounced	it	
were	called	jumped	
what	can	Kelly	**Knew**
would	cheered	learn	
you	cold	left	
	down	little	
	Drew	loud	
	Drew's	march	
	drink	my	
	few	need	
	fingers		
	finished		**new**

*Boldface words indicate sound-spelling introduced in this story.

When Drew finished the march, she jumped up. She flew outside to play with Artie and Kelly. They were tired and hot when Mother gave them a cold drink. "What a great practice we had!" they cheered.

"In a little bit," replied Drew. "I have to practice my new piano lesson. I want to learn the music."

"We can wait for a little bit," said Artie and Kelly.

"I have an idea!" said Drew. "I will play a march for you. You can try a few new moves. You can practice while I practice!"

"I knew Drew would help us!" said Kelly.

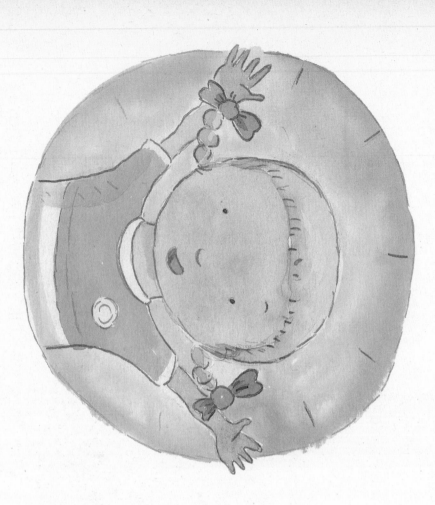

6

Drew played a few bars. The march grew loud and strong. Drew played with her right hand. With her left hand, she tapped the beat. On the beat, Artie threw the ball. Kelly bounced it back.

7

The Fruit Farm

by Molly Strong

illustrated by Holly Berry

"Girls, we are going to the fruit farm today," Mom says. "We will pick fruit to eat and to bake with. Lynn and Annie, you will help too! Change out of your swimsuits."

(continued)

Decodable Words

reaches	under
sit	us
swimsuits	very
takes	we
tell	will
that	with
the	won't
this	yellow
too	yes
tree	your
trees	

"What kind of fruit will we pick at the farm?" asked Annie.

"Yes, tell us what kind of fruit we will pick. Will we pick apples? Is it fruit to make juice with?" asked Lynn.

3

*Boldface words indicate sound-spelling introduced in this story.

"Is it fruit to make pies?" asked Annie.

"Mom, Mom! Is it fruit to make jellies? Is it fruit to make jam?" asked Lynn. "What kind of fruit are we going to pick?"

"The Fruit Farm"
Word Count: 241

High-Frequency Words	**Decodable Words**	
are	a	grow
from	and	help
into	Annie	
of	I	
says	apples	is
there	at	it
to	asked	
today	bake	jam
what	basket	jelly
you	big	jellies
	bite	**juice**
	but	**juicy**
	can	kind
	change	know
	dad	make
	each	mom
	eat	no
	farm	not
	fruit	now
	fuzzy	on
	girl	out
	girls	peach
	going	pick
		pies

*Boldface words indicate sound-spelling introduced in this story.

Dad says, "Guess what kind of fruit. It is yellow and very juicy, but we won't make juice from it. We will make pies and jam with it. Guess what fruit it is."

Lynn and Annie sit under the tree. There is a big fruit basket. Each girl reaches into the fruit basket and takes a big peach. Each girl takes a big juicy bite. Yum!

"I know what fruit it is!" says Annie. "I know too!" says Lynn. "Yellow pears grow on trees. We can make pies, and we can make jelly. We are going to pick yellow pears!"

"No," dad says. "The fruit that we are going to pick is not pears! This fruit is yellow and fuzzy, but we won't make juice from it. We will make pies and jam. Can you guess now?"

DECODABLE BOOK 15
Uncle Eddy's Suitcase

Uncle Eddy's Suitcase

by Marco Roberts

illustrated by Diane Paterson

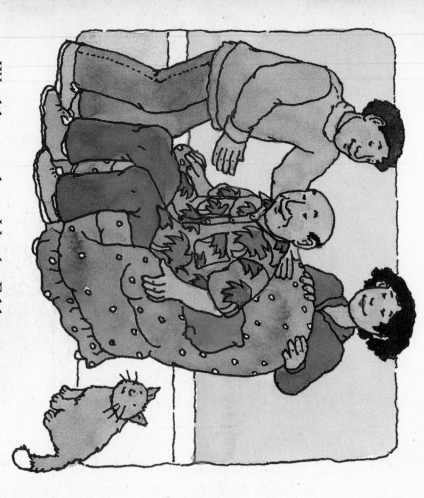

We like it when Uncle Eddy comes from Florida for a visit. He is so much fun! Mother and Father take his suitcase. They take him to a big chair. "Sit here, Uncle Eddy!"

2

(continued)

"Uncle Eddy, we have been recruited to take care of you!" say Alex and Tory.

"We want you to be happy. Can we bring you some juice?"

"That suits me just fine!" says Uncle Eddy.

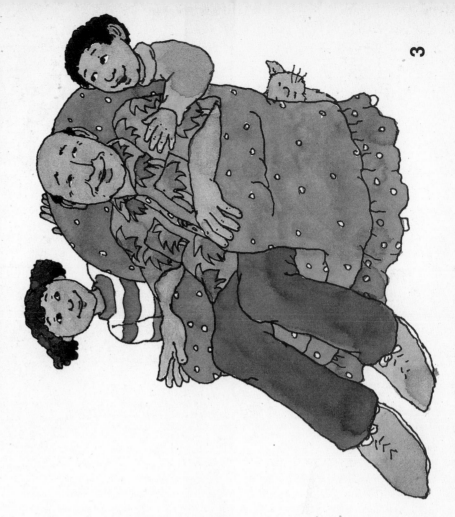

Decodable Words

so	uncle
suitcase	use
suits	visit
take	we
that	when
Tory	your

3

©Harcourt

*Boldface words indicate sound-spelling introduced in this story.

"Uncle Eddy's Suitcase"
Word Count: 235

High-Frequency Words

care	
comes	
from	
full	
have	
here	
of	
says	
some	
they	
to	
want	
what	
you	
you're	

Decodable Words

a	him
Alex	his
all	is
and	it
be	
big	
bring	**juice**
can	**juicy**
can't	just
Eddy	kind
Eddy's	like
fine	lime
	limes
for	make
fruit	me
fun	much
funny	my
get	please
happy	**recruited**
he	say
heavy	shall
	sit

Uncle Eddy says, "That suits me just fine."

"What kind of juice, Uncle Eddy? What kind of fruit shall we use to make your juice? Bananas? Shall we make banana juice?"

4

"Uncle Eddy, you're so funny! We can't make banana juice! What kind of fruit shall we use to make your juice? Watermelon? Shall we make watermelon juice?"

He says, "That suits me just fine!"

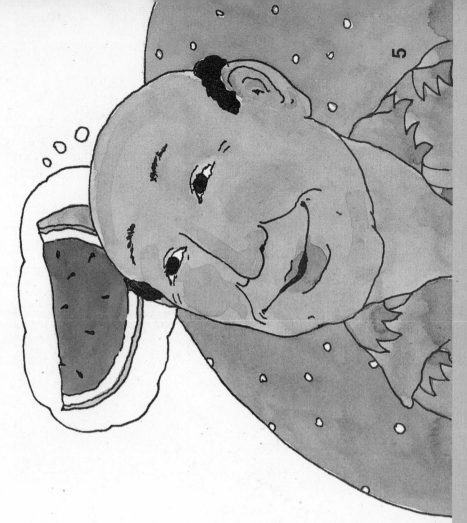

"What kind of juice shall we make?"
Uncle Eddy says, "Get my suitcase, please!"
His suitcase is heavy. It is full of big, juicy oranges!
Uncle Eddy says, "Shall we all make orange juice?"

"Uncle Eddy! You're so funny! We can't make watermelon juice! What kind of fruit shall we use? Pears? Shall we make you pear juice?"

Uncle Eddy says, "That suits me just fine!"

6

"Uncle Eddy! You're so funny! We can't make pear juice! What kind of fruit shall we use? Limes? Shall we make you lime juice?"

Uncle Eddy says, "That suits me just fine!"

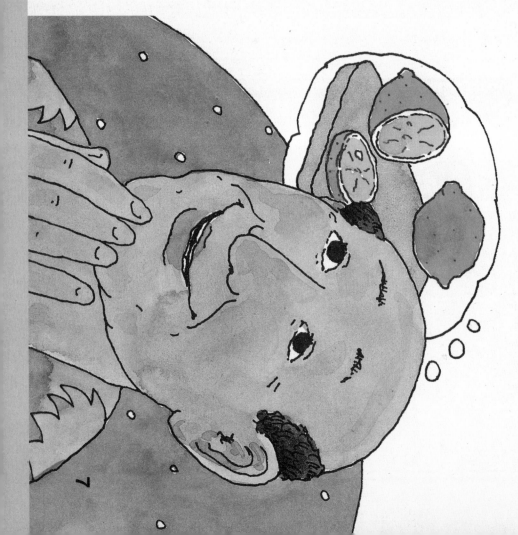

7

Rough and Tough Enough

by Daryll Jackson

illustrated by Viki Woodworth

"Come help me water the horses, Leroy," called Uncle Rusty. "The water trough is over there."

Leroy pumped water into the trough.

"Can I ride that horse?" Leroy asked, pointing to Patches.

2

(continued)

Uncle Rusty laughed. "Are you rough and tough enough?" he asked.

Leroy smiled also. "Of course I'm tough enough!" he cried. Still he wasn't really sure. Up close, the horses looked so big.

Decodable Words

pointing	so
pumped	still
really	stump
ride	that
riding	the
rode	then
rough	thinks
Rusty	told
saddle	**tough**
settled	trot
show	tumbled
showed	uncle
smiled	up
sneezed	very
snorted	water

*Boldface words indicate sound-spelling introduced in this story.

"First you have to show Patches
you are friendly." Uncle Rusty showed
Leroy how to hold an apple flat in
his hand. Patches took the apple. Leroy
gingerly patted the horse's rough hair.
Then he gave Patches a carrot.

"Rough and Tough Enough"
Word Count: 235

High-Frequency Words

about	
are	
around	
away	
come	
friendly	
from	
front	
have	
into	
looked	
of	
said	
sure	
there	
to	
took	
wasn't	
you	

Decodable Words

a	also	hand
an	and	hands
apple	help	he
as	himself	
asked	his	hold
backed	horse	
began	horse's	
big	horses	
by	how	
called	I	
can	I'm	
close	in	
course	is	
cried	it	
dust	just	
dusted	Leroy	
enough	Leroy's	
fell	mane	
felt	me	
fence	neck	
first	off	
flat	over	
gave	Patches	
gingerly	patted	

*Boldface words indicate sound-spelling introduced in this story.

Patches looked around and snorted. Leroy patted his neck. Patches began to trot.

"He thinks you are rough and tough enough," Uncle Rusty told Leroy. Leroy just smiled.

Patches backed away from Leroy and then sneezed. Leroy fell off the fence and tumbled into the dust. Uncle Rusty laughed.

"Are you rough and tough enough to ride Patches?" asked Uncle Rusty.

Leroy coughed as he dusted himself off. "Of course I'm tough enough!" Leroy said. He still wasn't sure about riding Patches. Up close, the horse looked very tough to ride.

Uncle Rusty rode Patches to the stump by the water trough. "Climb aboard!" he called. Leroy settled into the saddle in front of Uncle Rusty. He patted the horse's mane. It felt rough in Leroy's hands.

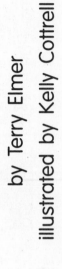

Patty's Tough New Jeans

by Terry Elmer

illustrated by Kelly Cottrell

DECODABLE BOOK 16
Patty's Tough New Jeans

"My goodness," said Mom. "You need new jeans."

Patty looked down. Her jeans were not long enough. She smiled and replied, "I guess I have been growing."

Mom and Patty went to the store.

2

(continued)

Patty tried on some jeans to find the right size. They all felt rough.

Mom said, "I know you like your old jeans better. We need to get some jeans that are long enough."

Decodable Words

new	spill
not	store
now	take
old	that
on	the
Patty	them
Patty's	think
perfect	**tough**
picking	tried
replied	up
right	used
rough	washed
scrapes	we
scratched	went
she	when
size	while
skate	wore
skating	your
smiled	

*Boldface words indicate sound-spelling introduced in this story.

"Patty's Tough New Jeans"

Word Count: 240

High-Frequency Words

	Decodable Words
about	a	getting
again	all	go
are	also	going
could	and	got
from	as	ground
goodness	be	growing
have	became	her
looked	berry	holes
said	berries	I
some	better	in
these	biking	inside
they	blue	it
to	close	jeans
useful	deep	just
was	dirt	kept
were	down	know
you	even	less
	enough	like
	fabric	long
	fell	lot
	felt	mom
	find	more
	fine	much
	for	my
	get	need

Patty's new jeans were long enough. They were also rough and tough. It was going to take a while to get used to them. She tried not to think about it.

4

©Harcourt

*Boldface words indicate sound-spelling introduced in this story.

Patty wore her new jeans to go skating.
When she fell down, the tough blue fabric
kept her from scrapes. She smiled when
she fell and got up to skate again.

Patty's new jeans were washed a lot.
The jeans became less rough-and-tough
and more like her old jeans. They even got
holes in them.

Patty smiled, "Now I like these jeans just
as much as my old jeans."

Patty wore her jeans berry picking. She could get close to the bushes and find berries deep inside.

The rough, tough jeans kept her from getting scratched. The long-enough jeans were useful.

Patty wore her new jeans to go biking. They were perfect for biking on rough ground. She could take a spill and be fine. She coughed from the dirt and got up again.

DECODABLE BOOK 16
Photos of Philly

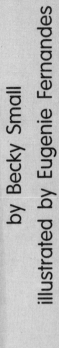

Photos of Philly

by Becky Small

illustrated by Eugenie Fernandes

1

When Phil and Phoebe came home from school, mom told them, "Uncle Walter Randolph phoned today. He asked us to come and visit. It has been a long time since we have seen the Randolphs."

(continued)

Decodable Words

Randolph	this
Randolphs	time
replied	told
see	uncle
seen	us
since	use
sit	visit
stay	Walter
still	we
take	went
that	when
the	will
them	won't
then	

"Let's get the photo album," said Phil.

"Let's look at the photos of the Randolphs," said Phoebe. "This book is heavy. It must be full of photos!"

"Look at this photo!" cried Phil.

*Boldface words indicate sound-spelling introduced in this story.

Phoebe told Phil, "We will see our cousins! We will see their new house. We will see their cat and dog!"

Phil replied, "The Randolphs will see us, but they won't see our cat!"

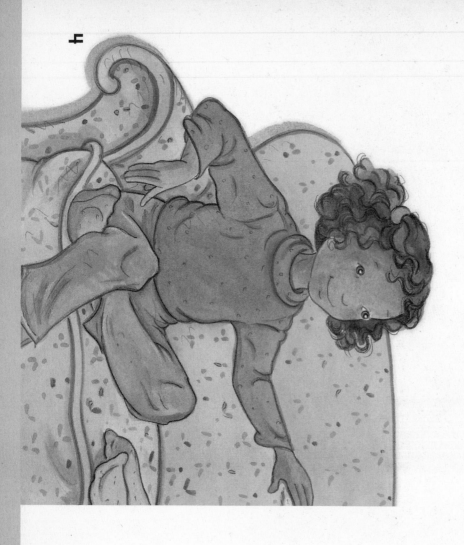

"Photos of Philly"
Word Count: 235
High-Frequency Words

	Decodable Words	
away	a	home
book	an	house
come	and	I
from	asked	if
full	at	is
great	be	it
have	but	let's
idea	called	long
look	came	make
of	can	mom
said	can't	must
school	cat	new
their	cried	not
they	did	now
to	dog	off
today	flash	our
want	for	**Phil**
you	get	**Philly**
	has	**phoned**
	he	**photo**
	heavy	**photos**
	held	plan
	her	ran

4

©Harcourt

Boldface words indicate sound-spelling introduced in this story.

"I have an idea," said Phil. "The Randolphs can't see our cat, Philly, but we can take a photo of Philly!"

"Great plan, Phil! Let's get the camera. Let's take photos of Philly!"

"Now we won't have a photo of Philly!" cried Phil. Phoebe said, "If Philly won't sit still for a photo, let's make a drawing of her. We can take them the drawing.

Phil and Phoebe called to their mom.
"Mom! Can we use the camera? We want
to take a photo of Philly."

"That is a great idea," Mom said. "You
can use it."

Phoebe held the camera and Phil held
the cat. Then Phil held the camera and
Phoebe held the cat. Philly did not want
to stay! When the flash went off, Philly
ran away.

Phipp Family Photo

by Cass Hollander

illustrated by Mike Tofanelli

One day, the Phipp family dressed in their best clothes. They were going to a special party. Mrs. Phipp wanted everyone to look nice. Mr. Phipp even wore his new green tie.

(continued)

Phil wore his best bow tie. Ralph wore his new pants. Mrs. Phipp took the boys downstairs to see their dad.

"We're beautiful!" cried Mrs. Phipp.

"Let's take a photo," said Mr. Phipp.

Decodable Words

not	stand
our	started
out	still
pants	take
party	the
Phil	them
Phipp	then
phone	those
photo	tie
photos	told
Ralph	too
replied	use
see	used
she	we
show	we're
so	went
sorry	wore

Boldface words indicate sound-spelling introduced in this story.

Mr. Phipp went to get the camera.

"Stand still for our photo," he told them.

Mrs. Phipp didn't stand still.

"Sorry. I thought I heard the phone," replied Mrs. Phipp.

"Phipp Family Photo"
Word Count: 237

High-Frequency Words	Decodable Words		
again	a	fly	
could	all	for	
everyone	and	funny	
family	asked	get	
good	ate	getting	
here	at	giggled	
look	be	going	
of	best	hard	
one	bow	he	
ones	boys	heard	
pictures	can	his	
said	clothes	how	
special	cried	I	
their	cut	if	
they	dad	in	
thought	day	is	
to	did	joke	
took	didn't	know	
wanted	don't	made	
were	downstairs	make	
you	dressed	new	
	enough	nice	
	even		

*Boldface words indicate sound-spelling introduced in this story.

Mrs. Phipp made one photo out of all the others. She cut apart the pictures. Mrs. Phipp used the best ones to make a family photo.

"Here is the Phipp family photo," she cried.

"Stand still for our photo," said Mr. Phipp again. Phil Phipp started to laugh. Ralph laughed, too.

"Sorry. I thought of a funny joke," giggled Phil.

"Please stand still," said Mrs. Phipp.

"Stand still. Don't laugh," said Mr. Phipp.
"How can we get a family photo if
you don't stand still?" he asked. Then Ralph
Phipp coughed and coughed.

"Sorry. I thought I ate a fly," said Ralph.

6

"Enough!" cried Mr. Phipp. "I did not
know getting one good photo could be so
hard!"

"Look at all those photos!" said Mrs.
Phipp. "I think I can use them to show
how nice we all look."

7

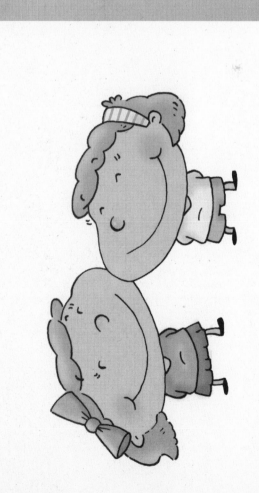

Blair and Claire Visit

by Dana Catharine

illustrated by Sarah Beise

1

Blair and Claire jumped out of bed.
This was a special day! They were going
to Grandma's house. Blair and Claire were
going on an airplane. The girls ran to the
window. The sky was clear and fair.

2

(continued)

The girls ran down the stairs to the kitchen. They sat down on the chairs at the table. Mom gave them plates piled high with pancakes.

Mom said, "Today we go on the airplane to Grandma's house!"

Decodable Words

packed	take
pair	the
pancakes	them
piled	then
plan	this
plates	three
ran	time
ready	told
sat	too
see	twins
shirts	**upstairs**
shorts	us
sit	visit
sky	we
smiled	will
so	window
socks	wings
soon	with
stairs	

*Boldface words indicate sound-spelling introduced in this story.

Blair and Claire were so happy! They would see Grandma. They would go on an airplane for the first time.

Mom told them, "Now go upstairs and get ready! What do you plan to take to Grandma's house?"

"Blair and Claire Visit"
Word Count: 247

High-Frequency Words	Decodable Words		
do	a	**air**	first
looked	of	**airplane**	fly
put		**airplane's**	for
said		**airport**	gave
special	all		get
their	an		giggled
they	and		girls
to	asked		go
today	at		going
took	bags		got
want	bed		happy
was	big		high
were	**Blair**		house
what	by		I
would	came		in
you	car		jumped
	cat		kitchen
	chairs		let's
	Claire		little
	clear		may
	cried		mom
	dad		my
	day		now
	down		on
	fair		out
			pack

©Harcourt

*Boldface words indicate sound-spelling introduced in this story.

Soon Dad, Mom, Claire, and Blair came to the airport. They took their bags. Blair and Claire looked at the big airplane and smiled. "This airplane will take us to Grandma's house."

"Let's pack," cried Blair. They got their little bags. "What shall we pack?"

"I packed my shorts, shirts, and three pair of socks!" said Claire. "Let's pack the cat, too!" giggled Blair. Mom smiled.

Dad put all the bags in the car. Then Mom and the twins got in the car, too. They were all ready to go to the airport.

"May I sit by the window?" asked Claire.

"May I sit by the window in the airplane?" asked Blair. "I want to see the airplane's wings! I want to see the airplane fly high in the air."

Grandma's Chair

by Bess Sanders

illustrated by Judy Stead

DECODABLE BOOK 17
Grandma's Chair

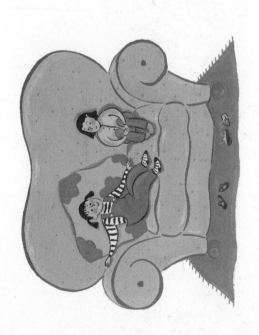

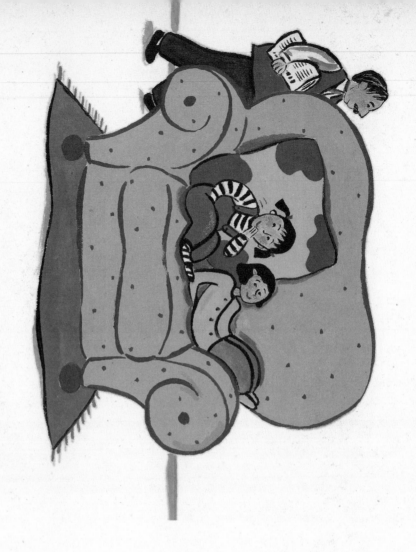

When Lucy and I go to Grandma's house, we like to sit in her chair. Grandma's chair is so big that the pair of us can sit in it together. We hide in Grandma's chair!

2

(continued)

Grandma's chair is upstairs. It is next to the window. In the summer, the warm air blows in the window. In the winter, it is cool. We creep into the chair with a blanket.

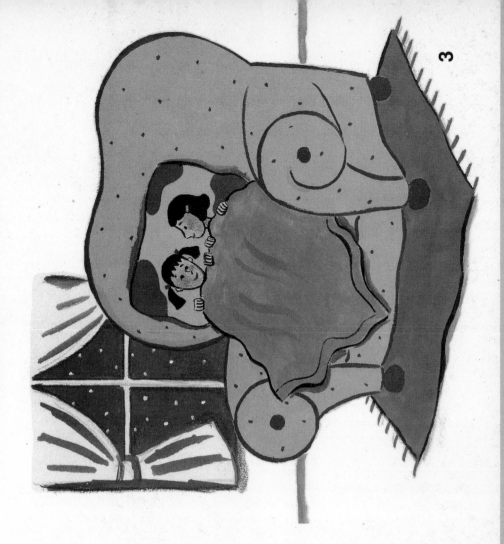

Decodable Words

not	summer
on	surprised
our	take
pair	tells
picks	that
pretends	the
read	then
reads	up
run	**upstairs**
set	us
she	wakes
side	warm
sit	we
sits	when
sleeping	window
snuggle	winter
so	with
stories	

*Boldface words indicate sound-spelling introduced in this story.

3

Grandma loves to sit in her chair and
read books. Sometimes she reads stories to us.
Grandma sits in the middle of her chair.
Lucy sits on one side, and I sit on the other.

"Grandma's Chair"
Word Count: 244
High-Frequency Words   **Decodable Words**

books	a	down
into	after	**downstairs**
love	all	eat
loves	**air**	end
of	and	**Fairy**
one	at	go
other	bath	**hair**
put	be	**Hairy**
sometimes	bed	he
to	big	help
together	blanket	her
	blows	hide
	both	his
	bows	house
	brush	I
	can	in
	carries	is
	cats	it
	chair	jump
	clean	know
	close	like
	cool	**longhair**
	creep	make
	day	middle
	dinner	next

*Boldface words indicate sound-spelling introduced in this story.

Sometimes Grandpa sits in Grandma's chair. He pretends that he is sleeping. We know that he is not sleeping! Lucy and I put bows in his hair. Then he wakes up and pretends to be surprised!

At the end of the day, after we eat, after we take a bath, and after we brush our hair, we like to run upstairs to Grandma's chair. Then we go to bed!

Grandpa picks us both up and carries us downstairs to Grandma. We help Grandma and Grandpa. We help make dinner. We set the table. Then we all eat together. Then we help clean up!

6

After dinner, Grandpa sits down with us on the sofa and tells us stories. Fairy and Hairy, the longhair cats, jump up and snuggle close to Grandpa. We love Grandpa and we love his stories!

7

Clare and Granny

by Beth Green

illustrated by Selina Alko

Clare was visiting at Granny's house today. Clare loved visiting with Granny. They always had fun together. Today they were going to bake a pie. Granny was a great baker and Clare was going to help!

(continued)

Decodable Words

peaches	spices
peel	**stared**
peeled	strips
pie	take
pies	than
plums	that
prepared	the
red	this
see	time
shall	visiting
share	waited
she	watch
smells	we
smiled	while
so	will
sort	with

"We have peaches, plums, and apples," said Granny. "What sort of pie shall we make?"

"Let's make an apple pie!" Clare said. Clare wanted to pare the apples and see the long strips of apple peel.

3

*Boldface words indicate sound-spelling introduced in this story.

Granny helped Clare pare the apples.

"Always watch what you are doing," said Granny. "Be careful."

Granny prepared the pie crust as Clare peeled the apples. Granny mixed sugar and spices and smiled at Clare.

4

"Clare and Granny"

Word Count: 249

High-Frequency Words	Decodable Words	
are	a	had
careful	air	help
doing	always	helped
family	an	her
great	and	house
have	apple	
love	apples	hugged
loved	as	is
of	asked	it
pictures	at	it's
said	bake	let's
they	baker	long
to	be	lots
today	big	make
together	**Clare**	made
wanted	crust	makes
was	drew	mark
were	filled	mixed
what	for	more
	fun	now
	going	our
	Granny	out
	Granny's	over
		pare

*Boldface words indicate sound-spelling introduced in this story.

"Clare!" said Granny. "It's time to take the pie out of the oven."

The smells of apples and cinnamon filled the air.

"Now," said Granny, "we will share the pie with our family."

Granny placed the crust over the apples. "Let's mark the pie with an 'A' for *apple*," Granny said.

"This is more than an apple pie. It's a Granny pie!" said Clare. Then Clare hugged her grandmother.

"What makes it a Granny pie?" asked Granny.

Clare said, "Granny pies are made with more than apples. They are made with love! This pie is made with lots of love, so it is a Granny pie!"

Clare drew pictures of big, red apples while she waited for the pie to be done. She drew lots of pies! She stared at the oven. She wanted that pie to be done!

A Picnic to Share

by Abe Beverly

illustrated by Burgandy Beam

DECODABLE BOOK 17
A Picnic to Share

I like to walk in the winter woods with Granny. The trees are bare. The leaves on the ground go crunch as we walk. We dare to have a picnic in the cold air!

2

(continued)

We watch the animals as we prepare our picnic. The rabbits and squirrels are scared. They must get ready for winter. There is no time to spare as they prepare for the cold.

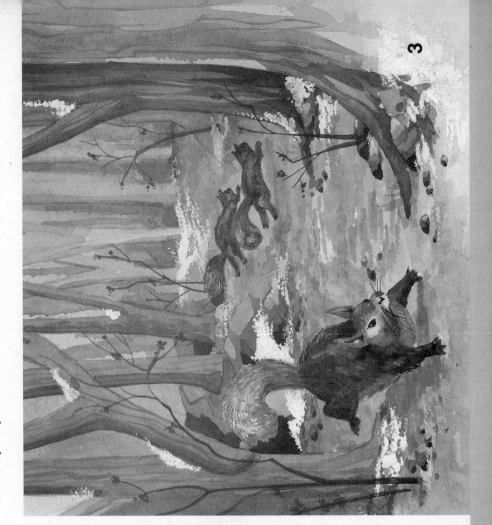

Decodable Words

makes	**share**
me	sit
must	sitting
my	**spare**
nice	**stare**
no	sun's
not	take
old	that
on	the
our	them
pick	then
picnic	think
prepare	those
prepared	time
quick	too
rabbits	tree
ready	trees
red	walk
sandwich	watch
sandwiches	we
scared	when
scares	winter
see	with

*Boldface words indicate sound-spelling introduced in this story.

We sit on an old tree. Granny and
I are prepared too. We share
sandwiches and hot chocolate. We eat
our winter picnic and stare as I drink
my chocolate carefully.

4

"A Picnic to Share"
Word Count: 239

High-Frequency Words

animals	
are	
carefully	
do	
have	
nothing	
of	
says	
there	
they	
to	
what	
you	

Decodable Words

a	for
after	get
air	**glare**
an	go
and	Granny
as	Granny's
at	ground
bare	hand
be	hang
berries	he
best	her
beware	hold
birds	home
branch	hot
branches	hungry
care	I
cold	icicles
crunch	in
dare	is
day	it
drink	leaves
eat	like
even	likes

*Boldface words indicate sound-spelling introduced in this story.

We are hungry when we get home after our winter picnic! Granny makes soup for a cold day. We share our day and our soup with Grandpa! What do you think he likes best?

8

A winter picnic must be quick! Even sitting in the sun's glare, it is cold in the woods! We share our sandwich crumbs with the birds. It is nice to take care of the animals in the woods.

5

We walk through the winter woods. We stare at the bare trees and the icicles that hang on the branches. I hold Granny's hand. When I hold her hand, nothing scares me!

6

The trees are bare. The branches are bare. Then what do we see! We see red berries on a branch and we do not pick them. Granny says, "Beware of those red berries."

7

How Much Wood?

by Wilbur Franco

illustrated by Jill Newton

DECODABLE BOOK 18
How Much Wood?

Fritz and Hans took a walk by the brook.

"Look at all that wood!" said Hans.

"How much wood would a woodchuck chuck if a woodchuck could chuck wood?" Fritz asked.

"You're silly!" said Hans. "Why would a woodchuck chuck wood? It might chew wood, but it wouldn't chuck wood!"

"Is wood good for a woodchuck to eat?" Fritz asked. "Can the woodchuck cook the wood?"

3

(continued)

Decodable Words

might	then
morning	think
mouth	**took**
much	us
must	use
my	walk
not	well
on	why
or	with
owl	**wood**
plants	**woodchuck**
she	**woodchucks**
shook	**woods**
silly	**wool**
so	**woolly**
stood	
tell	
that	
the	

*Boldface words indicate sound-spelling introduced in this story.

"Maybe woodchucks make wood cookies. They could use a cookbook to make cookies," Fritz said as he stood on one foot.

"Oh, Fritz! Woodchucks don't eat wood! Let's ask Owl. She lives in these woods."

4

"How Much Wood?"
Word Count: 245

High-Frequency Words		Decodable Words	
animal		a	**foot**
are		all	for
could		am	Fritz
do		an	go
lives		and	**good**
oh		as	Hans
one		ask	he
said		asked	head
saw		at	hear
something		beaver	her
these		**book**	how
they		branch	I
to		**brook**	if
was		but	in
would		by	it
wouldn't		called	its
you		can	just
you're		chew	know
		chuck	let
		cook	let's
		cookbook	**look**
		cookies	**looking**
		didn't	make
		don't	maybe
		eat	me

*Boldface words indicate sound-spelling introduced in this story.

©Harcourt

"Owl, tell us, please, do woodchucks eat wood or do they just chuck wood?" they asked.

"I don't know. Let me look in my book," said Owl. Then she shook her head. "Woodchucks eat plants," Owl said.

Fritz didn't hear. He was looking at something on a branch. "Look, Hans," he said. "Look, a woolly bear caterpillar. How much wool would a woolly bear bare if a woolly bear could bare wool?"

"Well, then woodchucks must chuck wood," said Fritz.

"I don't think so," said Hans. "Let's go ask a woodchuck." Fritz and Hans went to the brook. They saw an animal with wood in its mouth!

"Good morning," called Fritz. "Are you a woodchuck? Do you chuck wood? How much wood can you chuck?"

"I am not a woodchuck," said the animal. "I am a beaver. I don't chuck wood."

In the Woods

by Joan Sigmund

illustrated by Deborah Melmon

DECODABLE BOOK 18
In the Woods

The Perez family looked forward to summer camp. Summer camp was a good time to do nothing. They packed their car and left the city. They took their time driving to the camp.

2

(continued)

After she unpacked, Mrs. Perez put a chair by a babbling brook. She sat and read for hours. She did not have to stop and cook. At summer camp, the staff did all the cooking.

Decodable Words

near	**stood**
night	stop
not	suddenly
oars	summer
on	sun
over	swimming
packed	that
path	the
Perez	them
point	time
prints	too
read	**took**
rocky	top
rowboat	trail
rowed	unpacked
sat	up
see	waved
seen	went
setting	when
she	with
small	**woods**
so	wore
staff	

©Harcourt

Boldface words indicate sound-spelling introduced in this story.

"In the Woods"
Word Count: 245

High-Frequency Words

could
do
doesn't
family
from
have
hours
loved
nothing
put
said
their
they
to
two
was
were

Decodable Words

a	dock	
after	driving	
all	feel	
and	felt	
as	fire	
at	fish	
babbling	**fishhooks**	
back	fishing	
bedtime	for	
below	get	
by	**good**	
brook	got	
camp	had	
car	hike	
Carlos	**hoods**	
chair	**hoof**	
cheese	in	
chilly	it	
city	jackets	
cook	lake	
cooking	left	
crooked	**looked**	
deer	**lookout**	
did	made	
dinner	mud	

*Boldface words indicate sound-spelling introduced in this story.

Megan and Carlos took a hike in the woods. They climbed a trail for two hours to get to Lookout Point. The trail was crooked and rocky. From the top they could see the camp below.

4

Suddenly, a deer stood on the path.
Earlier they had seen his hoof prints in the
mud near the brook. When they got back
to camp, they went swimming in the lake.
It felt so good.

The camp staff made dinner over a fire.
Megan and Carlos wore their jackets with
hoods. It was chilly at night.

At bedtime, Mrs. Perez said, "Doesn't it
feel good to have nothing to do?"

Mr. Perez and Carlos were in a rowboat on the lake. Megan stood on the dock and waved. They looked up and waved back. Carlos took the oars and rowed toward Megan.

6

As the sun was setting, Mr. and Mrs. Perez went fishing on the lake. They put cheese on their fishhooks. The fish loved that! The fish looked too small so Mr. Perez put them back.

7

Could I Have Bubbles?

by Penny Tucker

illustrated by Esther Szegedy

DECODABLE BOOK 18
Could I Have Bubbles?

Doreen wanted to have that zest-zing feeling of being clean. She asked her mom, "Could I have some bubbles in my bath?"

Her mom called up the stairs, "Yes! You shouldn't use too much, though."

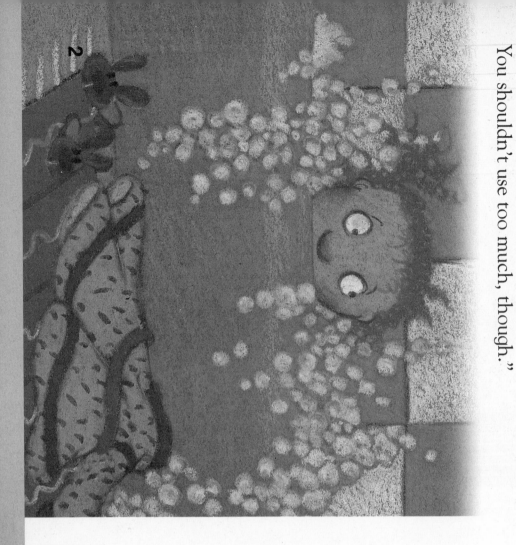

2

(continued)

Doreen poured the box of bubbles in her bath. She wanted to see the sparkle that would come from lots of bubbles. She did not think that a few bubbles over the side would be a problem.

Decodable Words

mom	soap
Mr.	soapy
much	sparkle
my	stairs
need	stand
next	stop
night	swirling
not	terrific
now	that
off	the
on	think
open	this
out	told
over	too
poured	understand
right	up
see	use
she	very
should	water
shouldn't	with
side	**would**
sidewalk	yard
slippery	yes
	zest
	zing

*Boldface words indicate sound-spelling introduced in this story.

"Should it be a problem? Could it be a problem?" wondered Doreen.

The bubbles and the foam flowed out on the floor and pushed open the door! The slippery soap lifted a night stand right off the floor.

"Could I Have Bubbles?"

Word Count: 243

High-Frequency Words

anymore
are
come
everywhere
from
have
of
some
someone
there
these
to
wanted
were
what
where
wondered
you

Decodable Words

a	and	flowed
	as	foam
		for
asked	bath	giggled
be		girl
being		glee
box		he
bubbles		help
		her
called		I
clean		I'll
cleanup		in
could		indeed
cried	dad	is
	did	it
	don't	jobs
	door	let
	Doreen	lifted
	drain	like
	end	lots
	feel	made
	feeling	**McCould**
	few	me
	floor	mess
		messy

*Boldface words indicate sound-spelling introduced in this story.

"Indeed, Mom, I feel terrific! I feel very clean and I don't need a bath anymore. I'll let the water drain out. Now, what would you like me to see?"

Where would the slippery soap stop? A girl on the sidewalk giggled with glee. Bubbles were swirling and as messy as could be.

Her dad told her, "Someone should clean these bubbles up."

Mr. McShould, next door, could not understand. He called for help. He cried, "Would someone please help? The bubbles are everywhere! My yard is covered with bubbles up to the door."

6

"Doreen," called her mom. "Would you, could you end this bath? You should be very clean. The bubbles have made a soapy mess. There are a few cleanup jobs I think you should see."

7

DECODABLE BOOK 18
Would You Like to Play?

Would You Like to Play?

by Richard Blake

illustrated by Barry Gott

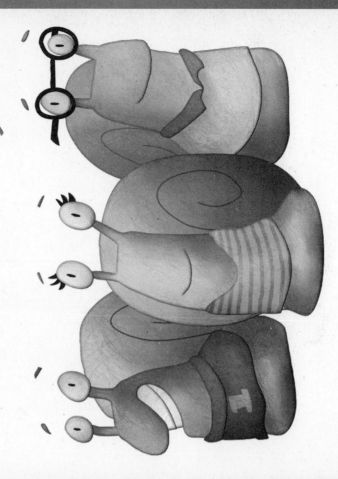

Jed, Tansy, and Albert Snail decided to play.

Jed asked, "What would you like to play? We could play checkers indoors again, but we should play outside because it is a sunny day."

2

Tansy replied, "It would be a good day to ride bikes."

"Yes," cried Jed. "We could play follow the leader on bikes. That sounds like fun."

Albert peered out of his glasses and told them, "We don't own bikes."

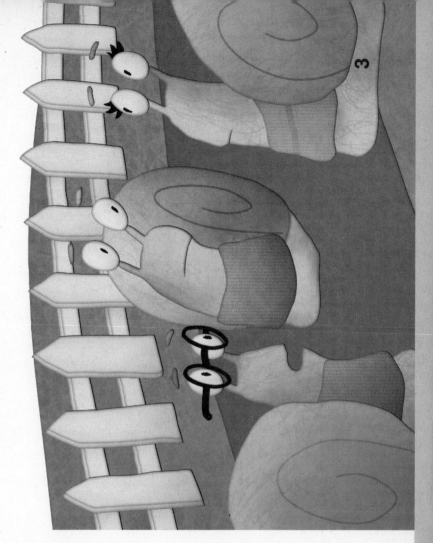

(continued)

Decodable Words

just	own	**should**	things
lake	peered	**shouldn't**	think
leader	perfect	snail	thinking
let	plane	so	this
like	plastic	sounds	told
little	play	started	us
mud	played	stop	water
my	playtime	stuck	way
no	quitting	sudden	we
not	rain	sunny	well
now	rained	Tansy	went
on	replied	that	when
our	riddles	the	**would**
out	ride	them	**wouldn't**
outside	shade	then	yes

*Boldface words indicate sound-spelling introduced in this story.

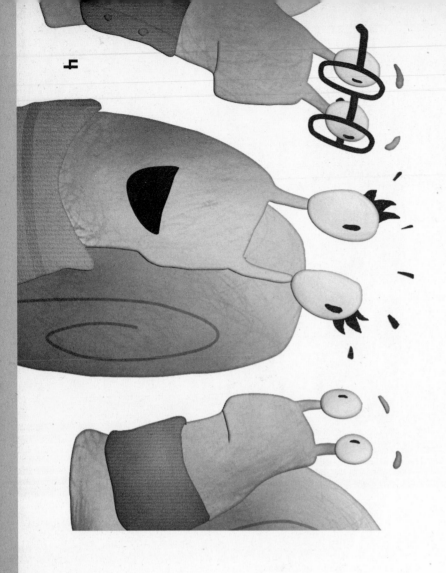

"Well, then," said Tansy, "we could play dolls in the shade."

"We could," replied Jed, "but some of us wouldn't like that. How about going down to the lake for a boat ride?"

4

"Would You Like to Play?"
Word Count: 248

High-Frequency Words	Decodable Words	
about	a	don't
again	afternoon	down
because	Albert	enough
do	all	flown
have	am	follow
of	and	for
oh	asked	fun
said	bat	game
some	be	get
sometimes	best	giggled
they	bikes	glasses
to	bit	going
what	boat	good
work	boating	got
you	book	had
	but	hard
	checkers	his
	could	how
	cried	I
	day	in
	decided	indoors
	deep	inside
	did	is
	dig	it
	dolls	Jed

*Boldface words indicate sound-spelling introduced in this story.

Jed, Albert, and Tansy did what they could when it rained. They went inside and played a game. They told riddles and giggled. They had a perfect afternoon. Sometimes, things just work out for the best.

8

"I don't think the water in that lake is deep enough. We would get stuck in the mud," said Albert.

"We could dig our way out. We shouldn't let a little bit of mud stop us," replied Tansy.

5

"No, no," said Albert. "Boating in the mud would not work."

Tansy cried, "I am thinking of quitting. Playtime should be fun. This is not! It is hard to agree."

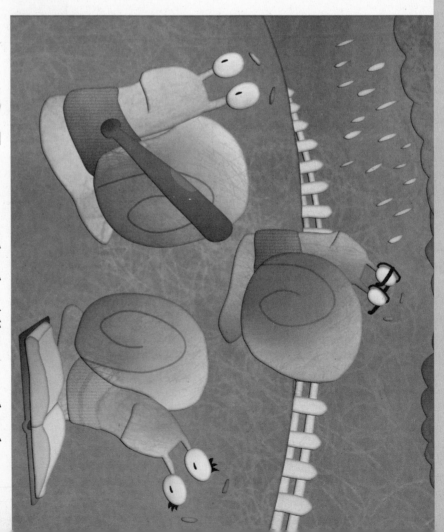

So Tansy got a book. Albert got his bat. All of a sudden, it started to rain.

"Oh, no, rain," cried Jed. "I should have flown my plastic plane. Now, what could we do?"

Lou's Routine

by Patsy Myers
illustrated by A.J. Garces

DECODABLE BOOK 19
Lou's Routine

Meet Lou Leary. Lou drives a city bus every day. He follows the same route from the airport to downtown and back. You would like Lou because he is so friendly. All the riders like Lou.

2

(continued)

Decodable Words

much	stores
name	take
new	tell
off	tells
on	thank
or	the
places	them
ridden	then
ride	this
riders	ticket
route	tickets
sales	tips
same	tours
say	try
seat	when
sell	will
sells	would
smiles	**you**
so	**you'd**
soup	**youth**
stop	

When you get on his bus, he will sell you a ticket. He sells two kinds of tickets. There are youth tickets and grownup tickets. He will say, "Thank you. Please take a seat. This bus is heading downtown."

Boldface words indicate sound-spelling introduced in this story.

Lou's routine is always the same. He will stop at every stop and let someone on or off. When you get off, he will say to you, "Have a good day." You can always count on Lou's being friendly.

"Lou's Routine"

Word Count: 259

High-Frequency Words		Decodable Words	
about	everyone	a	get
are	friendly	airport	good
because	from	all	**group**
every	give	always	grownup
	have	and	has
	of	at	he
	someone	ask	heading
	there	back	him
	they	be	his
	to	before	how
	two	being	if
	what	best	is
		boasts	kinds
		bring	know
		bus	knows
		can	Leary
		city	Leary's
		count	let
		courthouse	like
		day	likes
		downtown	**Lou**
		drives	**Lou's**
		eat	lunch
		fine	meet
		follows	meets
		for	

*Boldface words indicate sound-spelling introduced in this story.

You can tell when someone has ridden his bus before. They will know Lou Leary's name. They know the routine! Mr. Leary smiles and tells them what is new downtown. You'd be amazed at how much he knows.

Lou's routine is always the same. He follows the same bus route every day. He always has soup and salad for lunch. He is always friendly, and he likes everyone he meets.

Mr. Leary can tell you about the stores downtown having sales. He boasts about the fine courthouse, library, and museum. He likes to take group tours to the youth museum. They always bring back good souvenirs.

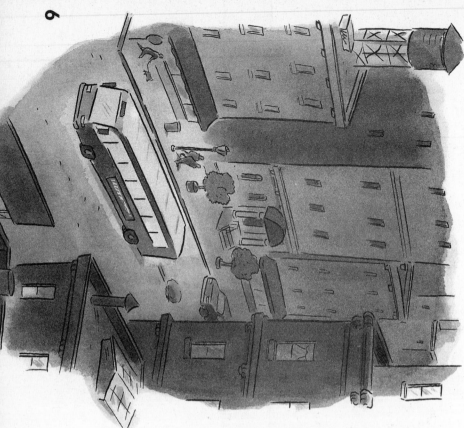

If you ride his bus, ask him about fine places to eat. He will give you tips on the best places. He will ask what you like. Then he will tell you good places to try.

Louise and Tommy Toucan

by Miles Hall

illustrated by Daniel Grant

DECODABLE BOOK 19
Louise and Tommy Toucan

Louise and Tommy Toucan came from the rain forests. From their youth, the birds lived in the zoo. The toucans lived in a group with other birds. They spent their days playing in the trees.

2

(continued)

Louise and Tommy were smart toucans.
The birds learned the routines of the zoo.
They knew that a man named Lou came
with food for them each day. The toucans
loved to eat all kinds of fruit.

3

Decodable Words

Louise	them
man	time
mixed	told
named	Tommy
never	**toucan**
nice	**toucans**
not	trees
off	us
playing	vet
rain	waited
reply	watched
same	when
say	will
see	with
smart	would
sorry	**wound**
soup	**you**
spent	your
stayed	**youth**
sweet	zoo
that	
the	

*Boldface words indicate sound-spelling introduced in this story.

The routine stayed the same. First the man fed the cougars. The big cats came down to the gate. When Louise and Tommy saw them cross their cage, it was time to eat.

4

"Louise and Tommy Toucan"
Word Count: 257
High-Frequency Words   **Decodable Words**

High-Frequency Words		Decodable Words		
because		a	big	food
come		all	birds	for
do		am	cage	forests
from		and	**group**	forget
here		at	going	fruit
lived		ate	had	
loved		beaks	he	
of		get	help	
one		gate	his	
other			hurt	
said				
saw		cats	I	
their		came	in	
they		called	is	
to		cross	it	
two		day		
was		days	juice	
were		did	kinds	
		down	knew	
		dribble	last	
		each	learned	
		eat	long	
		fed	**Lou**	
		finally		
		first		
		fix		

*Boldface words indicate sound-spelling introduced in this story.

Finally Lou came. He told the toucans, "I am sorry, you two nice birds. One of the cougars was hurt, and I had to get help. The vet will fix his wound. I would never forget you."

Tommy would say, "Do you see the cougars at the gate?"

Louise would reply, "Tommy, it is not time to eat." When the toucans saw the big cats going to their gate, they knew their sweet fruit would come.

Lou would say, "Here is your fruit soup." He called it fruit soup because the fruit was mixed with juice. The toucans ate the fruit, and the juice would dribble off their beaks.

One day the routine was not the same. Louise and Tommy watched the cougars. They waited a long time. At last the big cats came down to their gate. "You see, Tommy," said Louise. "Lou did not forget us."

6

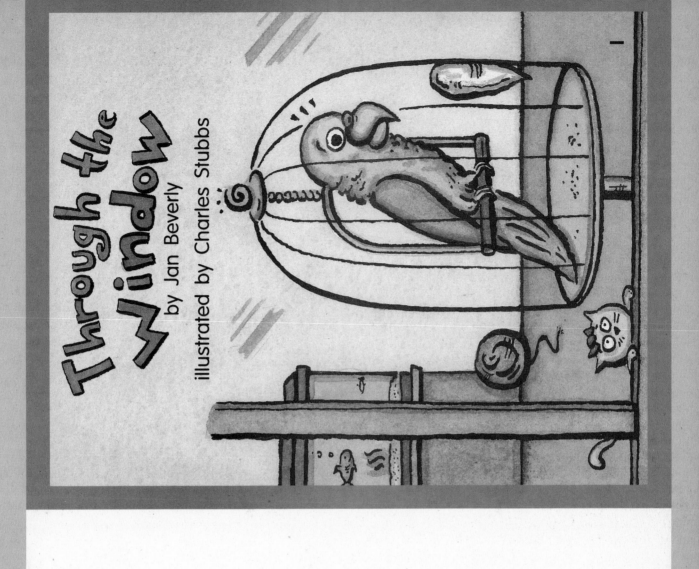

Through the Window

by Jan Beverly

illustrated by Charles Stubbs

DECODABLE BOOK 19
Through the Window

Throughout the day Arthur sat on a perch in the pet shop window. He looked through the glass at the people who walked by. Arthur did not move from his perch.

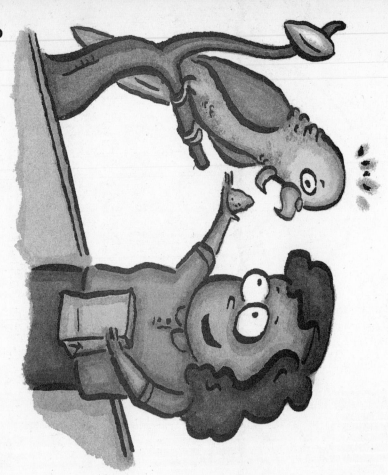

People looked through the pet shop window to see the pets. Sadly, Arthur did not know many words. He screeched, "Scram! Strike one!" People did not think Arthur was very friendly.

Decodable Words

now	strike
nuts	strong
on	stuck
or	tail
out	tangles
Pam	that
perch	the
pet	think
pets	**through**
ran	**throughout**
running	told
sadly	turned
sat	twisted
scram	used
screeched	very
see	walked
she	watched
shop	wave
slick	when
slid	window
smile	wings
so	with
sound	yarn
still	**you**
stop	

(continued)

*Boldface words indicate sound-spelling introduced in this story.

Arthur was friendly though. Ellen was his good friend. Ellen was a frisky kitten that everyone loved. Arthur was fond of Ellen because she made him smile. Ellen ran through the pet shop chasing her tail or a yarn ball.

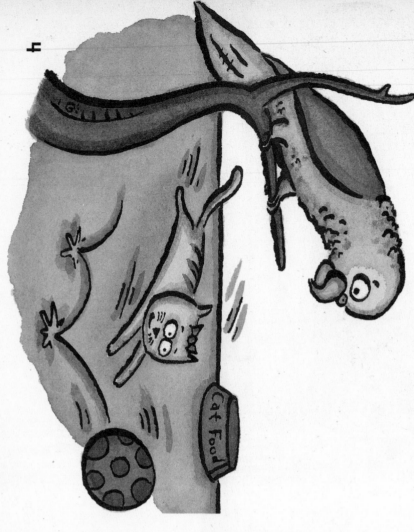

"Through the Window"

Word Count: 245

High-Frequency Words

because
could
doesn't
everyone
friend
friendly
from
loved
many
move
of
one
people
put
said
says
they
to
was
what

Decodable Words

a
after
almost
and
Arthur
at
ball
beak
bird
by
came
can
chasing
clip
crack
cried
day
did
door
down
Ellen
even
fast
flew
floor
flutter

fond
free
frisky
fun
get
glass
good
had
he
help
her
him
his
I
if
in
is
kitten
know
look
looked
made
me
more
not

*Boldface words indicate sound-spelling introduced in this story.

©Harcourt

One day Ellen was having fun running after her yarn. She ran so fast that she slid on the slick floor. She almost flew through the door. She put out her claws to stop.

Pam told everyone what Arthur had done. Now when people look through the glass, they wave at Arthur. He still says, "Scram!" People now know that he is a very good bird even though he doesn't sound friendly.

One day, Arthur watched Ellen get stuck in her yarn ball. She could not get through the tangles. The more she twisted and turned, the more stuck she was. She cried, "Arthur, help me!"

Arthur said, "Ellen, if I can crack nuts, I can free you." With a flutter of his wings, Arthur came down from his perch. Arthur used his strong beak to clip through the yarn.

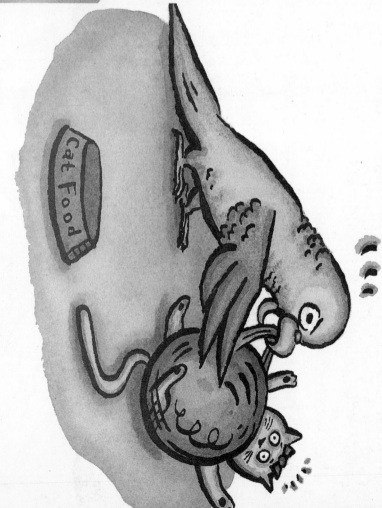

Swogs Throughout

by Rob Sherlock

illustrated by Christiane Beauregard

DECODABLE BOOK 19
Swogs Throughout

I am going on a Swog hunt through the woods. My plastic boots are good if I have to go in the slough. The slough is the creek in the marsh.

2

What I am hunting for are Swogs. A Swog is an animal that is part dog, part duck, and part giraffe. Swogs are very funny looking and hard to find. They hide throughout the woods and anywhere they want.

(continued)

Decodable Words

looking	the
marsh	them
me	think
mud	this
my	**through**
never	**throughout**
on	time
part	tracks
peeking	tree
perhaps	trees
place	under
plastic	very
see	why
slough	will
slow	window
steps	woods
Swog	would
Swogs	writing
teacher's	you
that	

*Boldface words indicate sound-spelling introduced in this story.

Swogs belong in the woods, but they like to wander. That is why you never know where you will find one. One time I saw a Swog peeking through a window in an empty classroom!

4

"Swogs Throughout"
Word Count: 253
High-Frequency Words

animal
another
anywhere
are
around
gone
have
here
into
of
one
saw
some
there
these
they
to
want
was
were
what
where

Decodable Words

a
air
am
an
and
before
belong
board
boots
but
by
can
classroom
close
could
creek
desk
did
dog
down
duck
empty
end
even
feeling
find

fly
follow
for
funny
glasses
go
going
good
happened
hard
hide
hiding
hollow
hunt
hunting
I
if
in
is
just
know
leaves
like
log
look
looked

*Boldface words indicate sound-spelling introduced in this story.

©Harcourt

This is a good place to look around. One could have gone through the hollow log here. I could even look through the leaves of this tree. If they would just slow down, I know I could find one.

$2+6=8$

I climbed the steps. I looked through that classroom window. There was a Swog writing on the board. Another one was hiding under the teacher's desk. The Swogs were throughout the classrooms.

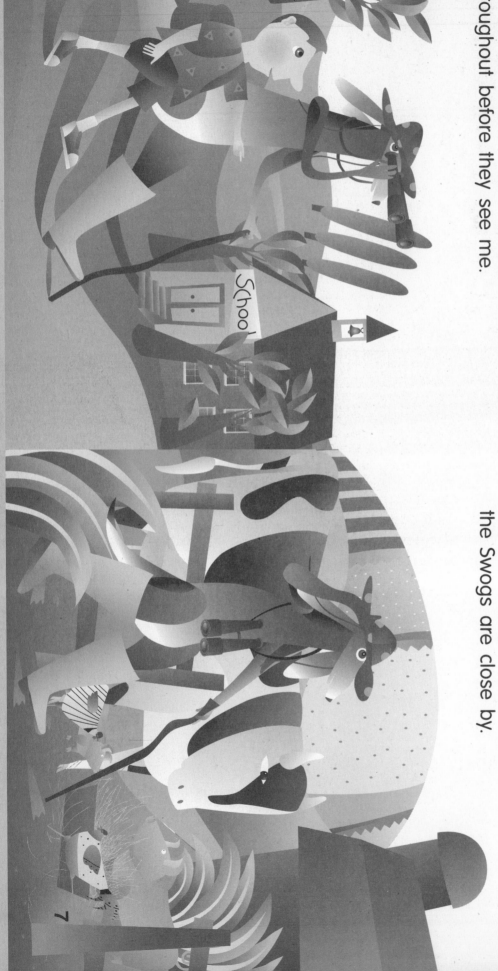

I think I can find the Swogs by looking through these glasses. Perhaps I will find some Swog tracks in the mud here. I can follow them and find the Swogs hiding throughout before they see me.

The tracks end here by the trough. What happened? Where did the Swogs go? If they are part duck, can they fly through the air and into the trees? I have a feeling the Swogs are close by.

6

7

Night Crawler Fishing

by Elmer Richards

illustrated by Robin Moro

DECODABLE BOOK 20
Night Crawler Fishing

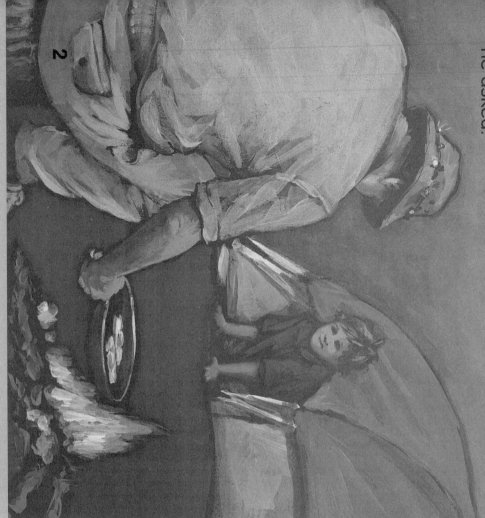

Andy yawned as he crawled out of the tent. His dad was cooking eggs over the campfire at dawn.

"Are you and Reed ready to start fishing?" he asked.

2

They walked down the dirt road.

"Look, Andy," Reed yelled. "There's a hawk with a mouse in its claws." Andy was glad his best friend could come fishing for the first time with him.

(continued)

Decodable Words

his	night	slow	those
holding	on	spots	time
hungry	only	**sprawled**	tired
I	out	start	told
icebox	over	still	trees
in	**raw**	**tawny**	waited
it	ready	tent	walked
its	Reed	that	we
jaw	road	**thaw**	whispered
know	rod	the	white
lake	rubbed	them	with
landed	running	there's	**yawn**
law	see	thick	**yawned**
lift	set	thing	**yawning**
lit	**shawl**	think	yelled
look	show	this	you
mouse	slipped		

*Boldface words indicate sound-spelling introduced in this story.

©Harcourt

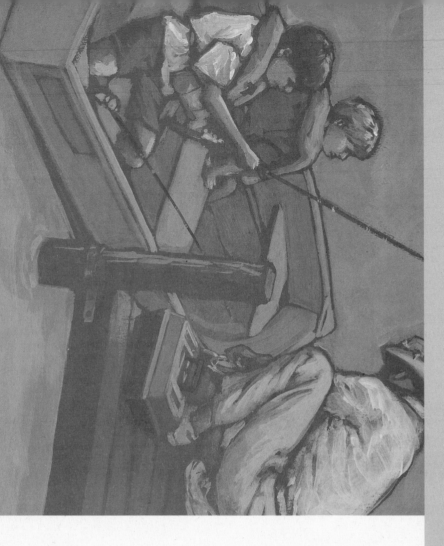

"Do you boys want to drive this boat?"
asked Andy's dad with a yawn.

"Sure!" they both said. They set out on the
lake at a slow crawl. "Can't this thing go any
faster?" asked Reed.

"Night Crawler Fishing"
Word Count: 254

High-Frequency Words		Decodable Words			
any		a	and	dad	
are		and	Andy	**dawn**	
come		do	Dean	deer	
do		as	Andy's	didn't	
friend		at	asked	dirt	
have		be	down	**draw**	
into		big	best	drive	
of		boat	eggs		
one		both	faster	**fawn**	
onto		boys	fell		
put		by	first		
said		called	fish		
says		campfire	fishing		
some		can	five		
sure		can't	**flaw**		
they		catfish	for		
to		**claws**	forgot		
tonight		cooking	glad		
want		could	go		
was		**crawl**	has		
what		**crawled**	**hawk**		
where		**crawler**	he		
		crawlers	him		

Boldface words indicate sound-spelling introduced in this story.

"Hey, Dad," said Andy, "we forgot to lift the anchor!"

Mr. Dean laughed and rubbed his jaw.

"I told you, boys. You are running this show."

"The law says you can only have five fish," Andy told Reed.

Andy and Reed put a thick shawl on as Mr. Dean lit the campfire.

"What do you think of fishing?" Andy asked.

"It has only one flaw," said Reed, yawning.

"I didn't know I could be this tired."

They waited for the night crawlers to draw the hungry catfish. "Look! I see a fawn and some deer by those trees," Reed whispered.

"Where?" called Andy.

"See that tawny color with white spots?" Reed answered.

6

"I think I landed a big one!" yelled Andy. He fell, sprawled out on the bottom of the boat. He was still holding on to the rod.

Mr. Dean slipped the raw fish into the icebox. "We can thaw them tonight."

7

What Shelby Saw!

by Allen Chester

illustrated by Janet Montecalvo

DECODABLE BOOK 20
What Shelby Saw!

"Shelby, time to feed the dog! We don't want your dog to go hungry," her mom called. Shelby stopped drawing and went to find Sammy in the backyard. The yellow lab was gnawing on a raw bone.

2

Sammy ran to Shelby from across
the lawn. He put his paws on her
arms eagerly.

"Good boy," she said, patting his head.

Sammy happily chomped on the dog food.

(continued)

Decodable Words

I	on	**saw**	think
if	only	see	time
in	open	seemed	told
jaw	out	send	under
kittens	over	she	up
lab	patting	Shelby	walked
lawn	**paw**	Shelby's	we
led	**paws**	Skyler	we'd
look	pet	Skyler's	went
lost	prints	smart	when
missed	ran	so	without
mom	**raw**	**sprawled**	**yawned**
morning	returned	stopped	yellow
Mrs.	room	surprise	you
muddy	rug	taking	you'll
new	run	the	your
next	sadly	them	
no	Sammy	there's	

*Boldface words indicate sound-spelling introduced in this story.

"Oh no!" Shelby cried. "There's a new hole under the fence." She didn't want Sammy to crawl out and run away.

"Don't move," she told Sammy. She went to look for something to fill up the hole.

©Harcourt

"What Shelby Saw!"
Word Count: 255

High-Frequency Words	Decodable Words	
around	a	eagerly
away	and	empty
come	arms	feed
from	as	fence
gone	at	fill
move	backyard	find
of	began	fixed
oh	**bawl**	**flaw**
put	begged	food
said	bone	for
something	boy	**gnawing**
their	by	go
there	called	good
these	care	had
thought	chomped	he
to	**crawl**	head
want	cried	helped
was	curled	her
were	**dawn**	him
what	didn't	his
	dog	hole
	don't	home
	door	house
	drawing	hugged
	drawings	hungry
	dropped	

*Boldface words indicate sound-spelling introduced in this story.

When Shelby returned, her jaw dropped open in surprise. Muddy paw prints led under the fence. Sammy was gone. Shelby began to bawl. Her mom helped her put up drawings for a lost dog by their house.

Shelby walked to Mrs. Skyler's lawn to see the kittens. There was Sammy sprawled around them!

"Oh, you smart watchdog!" she said as she hugged him. "You were taking care of these kittens!"

The next morning at dawn Shelby yawned. She missed her pet.

"If only we'd fixed the flaw in the fence," she thought sadly. Her room seemed so empty without Sammy curled up on the rug. "Sammy, come home," she begged.

The lady next door, Mrs. Skyler, had new baby kittens. Mrs. Skyler told Shelby's mom to send her over.

She said to Shelby, "I think you'll be surprised by what I saw." Shelby still missed her dog Sammy.

Mrs. McNaught's Field Trip

by Marcel Black

illustrated by Rusty Fletcher

DECODABLE BOOK 20
Mrs. McNaught's Field Trip

Mrs. McNaught said, "I am the daughter of a man who drove trains. You ought to know more about trains. I am your teacher, and I will tell you what he taught me."

(continued)

Decodable Words

my	that
near	the
on	them
or	things
places	this
quiet	time
railroad	told
railroads	tracks
read	train
remember	trains
ride	trip
sail	turn
sailboats	used
sailing	water
see	went
she	when
sight	why
signs	will
song	wind
street	yard
taught	you
teacher	your
tell	

Mrs. McNaught and her class caught a bus. When everyone was quiet, the driver said, "I remember when my daughter was in Mrs. McNaught's class." Then the driver told them how he used a map and read the street signs.

3

*Boldface words indicate sound-spelling introduced in this story.

Mrs. McNaught said, "Look at the sailboats. See how fast they can go after the sail has caught the wind! Mr. McNaught taught me how to turn the sail to catch the wind."

"Mrs. McNaught's Field Trip"

Word Count: 255

High-Frequency Words

about	
again	
all	
brought	
everyone	
faraway	
of	
said	
school	
they	
to	
was	
were	
what	
where	
who	
working	

Decodable Words

a	go	
after	got	
all	had	
am	has	
and	he	
asked	her	
at	hike	
back	how	
bay	I	
boat	in	
boys	it	
bus	kinds	
can	know	
cars	liked	
caught	long	
class	look	
daughter	looked	
dreaming	lunch	
driver	man	
driving	map	
drove	**McNaught**	
fast	**McNaught's**	
field	me	
for	more	
girls		

*Boldface words indicate sound-spelling introduced in this story.

When they got to the railroad yard, the class looked at all the trains. Mrs. McNaught taught the class about the kinds of cars. The boys and girls liked to read where the trains had been.

It was a long ride back to school. Mrs. McNaught had taught the class about things that go. The boys and girls were caught dreaming of sailing a boat or driving a bus or train.

The class went for a hike after lunch. They caught sight of the bay and the sailboats again. Mrs. McNaught taught them why the train tracks were near the water. "Trains brought things to faraway places," she said.

The class caught the bus again to go back to school. This time the driver asked the boys and girls to read the street signs. Mrs. McNaught taught them a song about working on the railroads.

The Naughty Bunny

by Robert Norris

illustrated by Amanda Haley

DECODABLE BOOK 20
The Naughty Bunny

Mrs. Buttercup and her daughter Ann went to the pet store to pick out a rabbit. The baby rabbits were so cute that it was hard to pick. The store owner caught one for Ann to hold.

2

(continued)

Ann picked the blond rabbit because he
was the curious one. The rabbit sniffed
Ann's hand and licked it.
"I will name him Laughton," said Ann.
The store owner caught Laughton again
and put him in a box for Ann.

3

Decodable Words

licked	so
liked	stayed
make	stop
name	stopped
naughty	store
needed	**taught**
next	teach
not	teeth
now	that
on	the
out	things
owner	under
pet	until
pick	up
picked	went
rabbit	will
rabbits	wire
right	with
rocks	wooden
safe	wrong
sharp	yard
she	you
sniffed	your

*Boldface words indicate sound-spelling introduced in this story.

He said, "Your mother taught you right and wrong. Now it is up to you to teach Laughton. Help him grow up to be a good pet. Don't let him be a naughty bunny."

4

©Harcourt

"The Naughty Bunny"
Word Count: 257

High-Frequency Words

again	
another	
are	
around	
because	
doing	
from	
many	
one	
put	
said	
they	
to	
was	
were	
where	

Decodable Words

a	after	Field's
and	for	garden
Ann	get	good
be	grow	grass
being	hand	
blond	hard	
box	he	
bunny	help	
Buttercup	her	
cat	him	
caught	his	
chewed	hold	
chewing	hole	
chew	hopped	
chicken	I	
could	in	
cute	is	
daughter	it	
day	keep	
dig	**Laughton**	
don't	legs	
door	let	
dug		
eating		
fence		

*Boldface words indicate sound-spelling introduced in this story.

Ann taught Laughton many things. She could not teach Laughton to stop chewing things. Laughton needed to chew things to keep his teeth sharp. Laughton chewed table legs and shoes.

"You are a naughty bunny," said Ann.

Mrs. Buttercup taught Ann to make the yard safe for Laughton. They put chicken wire around the carrots. They put rocks where Laughton liked to dig under the fence. After that, Laughton stopped being a naughty bunny.

Ann taught Laughton to get along with Mrs. Field's cat next door. Laughton stayed curious. He dug a hole under the wooden fence. He hopped on the grass next door until Ann caught him.

6

Another day Ann caught Laughton eating carrots from Mr. Carson's garden. "You are a naughty bunny, Laughton," said Ann. Mrs. Buttercup said, "Ann, Laughton is a rabbit doing 'rabbit things.' He is not being naughty."

7